D1613976

JEEP
CJ to Grand Cherokee

JEEP
CJ to Grand Cherokee

A collector's guide
by James Taylor

MOTOR RACING PUBLICATIONS LTD
Unit 6, The Pilton Estate, 46 Pitlake, Croydon CR0 3RY, England

First published 1999

British Library Cataloguing in Publication Data

Taylor, James, 1950-
    Jeep : CJ to Grand Cherokee. - (Collector's guide)
    1. Jeep automobile - History
    I. Title
    629.2'22

ISBN 1-899870-33-4

Printed in Great Britain by
The Amadeus Press Ltd
Huddersfield, West Yorkshire

Contents

Introduction and acknowledgements

I was delighted when MRP's John Blunsden agreed with me that the time was right for the *Collector's Guide* series to include a volume on Jeep. To my knowledge and his, there was no book among the large number published on the subject which treated the marque in the systematic historical fashion characteristic of this series, and we both thought such a book was long overdue.

We also knew that cramming nearly 60 years of Jeep development between these covers would present a few problems, and on that score we were both right! So at the outset, let me point out that space restrictions are the reason why I have treated the definition of Jeep very strictly here. This means that the book does not cover models built by AM General, the AMC subsidiary responsible for the Mighty Mite of the 1960s (often called a Jeep) and the current Hummer. Space also means that it simply hasn't been possible to record every single permutation of every model. It has always been a Jeep characteristic to offer a vast range of accessories and options, and it would take a book many times the size of this one to record them all. (It would also make pretty boring reading, but that's another story.) And, yes – many Jeep owners do personalize their vehicles to a large extent. This book doesn't attempt to delve into that side of the story. All you'll find here are thoroughbred Jeeps, beginning with the wartime MB and going on through to today's luxury wagons.

Readers familiar with the *Collector's Guide* series may notice the absence from this book of the comprehensive buying and ownership chapter which characterizes other volumes in the series. The reason for this is that the huge diversity of Jeep models and types means that for the job to be done thoroughly would require a book in itself. Therefore, in this instance we confine ourselves to a few words of general advice to buyers of Jeeps of all ages and in all countries: we strongly recommend that your first priority when buying a vehicle is to locate and befriend your local Jeep specialist, franchised or otherwise. Specialists and enthusiasts' clubs regularly advertise in the 4x4 magazines, so we suggest that your search should start there.

We both hope that this book does justice to the marque which originated the modern lightweight 4x4. There will inevitably be some mistakes and omissions, for which I willingly accept responsibility, but I do hope there are not too many of either. I certainly can't place any blame on the people who helped me out while I was writing the book. In alphabetical order (thus, no favouritism), they are Mark Askew (*Jeep World*), John Carroll (*Toledo Telegraph*), Robin Craig, Richard Howell Thomas (*International Off-Roader*), Tom Johnston (Chrysler Jeep UK Press Office), Patrick Kear (Yankee Jeep Club) and Clive Sweet (Brooklands Books). Thanks are also due to the guys at MRP who held their breath and kept their fingers crossed as the deadline for finishing this book was approaching.

James Taylor

Who has owned the Jeep name?
1941-1954   Willys Overland Company, Toledo, Ohio
1954-1970   Kaiser Industries
             Note: The company was still known as Willys Overland until 1963, when its name was changed to Kaiser Jeep Corporation.
1970-1987   American Motors Corporation, Detroit, Michigan
1987 on   Chrysler Corporation, Detroit, Michigan

CHAPTER 1

The military Jeep

MA to MD and others

The Jeep's image of rugged dependability derives from the marque's origins as a purely military vehicle, although today's Jeeps have come a very long way indeed from the crude vehicle which was the first to bear the name back in 1941. Exactly where that name came from, incidentally, has never been proven beyond doubt. However, it was certainly popularized by journalist Katharine Hillyer, who heard it from test driver Red Hausmann and used it in the Washington *Daily News* during February 1941.

There are two theories about how Hausmann found it. It was either a slurring of the initials GP, which stood for General Purpose or, more romantically, it was borrowed from E C Segar's Popeye cartoon. Eugene the Jeep was a character in the cartoon, and the little creature had the ability to go anywhere at will. The new quarter-ton truck prototypes seemed to have that same ability, and the nickname would have been used by military staff putting them through their paces at the US Army's Camp Holabird test ground.

During the 1920s and 1930s, the US Army had experimented with a number of cross-country vehicles, which were intended to improve its mobility over rough terrain. Among these, the most successful were probably conversions of standard commercial light trucks, which had four-wheel drive to provide the necessary traction. However, all attempts to come up with a small and manoeuvrable runabout which could be used for reconnaissance and general light transport duties had failed. Nevertheless, the US Army was convinced of the necessity for such a vehicle.

So it was that when war broke out in Europe during September 1939, and it began to look as if the USA would eventually get sucked into the conflict, the US Army renewed its efforts to develop an all-terrain runabout.

The American Quartermaster Corps Technical Committee began to focus on the issue in the summer of 1940. On June 27, it issued a set of requirements for such a vehicle, inviting US motor manufacturers to meet an impossibly tight deadline of July 22 for the submission of designs and demanding 70 prototypes within 75 days subsequent to that.

More than 135 motor manufacturers were invited to submit designs for the new military all-terrain runabout, which had to have four-wheel drive, a wheelbase of 80 inches and a payload of 600lb, and meet certain speed criteria and a very low weight limit. But the deadlines were incredibly tight, and there seemed to be little pressure because the US was not yet at war, so just two companies took the trouble to prepare designs. Those companies were American Bantam and Willys Overland. Both of them had been successful makers of small cars, but they were now looking for new and lucrative contracts to shore up the beginnings of decline. Bantam, in particular, was in desperate straits.

Nevertheless, the Bantam and Willys Overland representatives who attended at Camp Holabird to submit their designs on July 22, 1940 found that they were not alone. Crosley, another maker of small cars, and Ford had both sent representatives as observers, reasoning that they

Most of the 1,500 Bantam BRC-40 models were used by America's allies. This example was pictured in service with the British 6th Armoured Division. Note the skid-plates under the centre of the chassis.

might stand a chance if the deadline had proved too tight for anyone else to come up with a design. Crosley soon faded from the picture, but Ford would go on to play a major part in the story of the Jeep.

The Willys Overland design was really little more than an outline sketch, and the company wanted to extend the time allowed for building a first prototype. However, the Bantam proposal was well-executed and was complete. So even though Bantam's costs were higher than those proposed by Willys, the Quartermaster Corps favoured their proposal and asked them to go ahead and build the prototype batch of 70 vehicles. The first was delivered to Camp Holabird for testing on September 23, just half an hour before the expiry of the deadline for its submission set by the Army.

This Bantam was to prove the basis for the eventual production Jeep, and it is worth noting that it had been designed in two and a half days by a consulting engineer called Karl K Probst, whom Bantam had hired specifically for the job. It was based to a large extent on existing componentry, with a reinforced version of a Bantam roadster chassis which had earlier been submitted for military approval and rejected, with a bought-in Continental four-cylinder engine, and Spicer axles and transmission components. The doorless steel body tub was as basic as it could be, the front wings were little more than splash guards, and the weight was well above the limit set by the Quartermaster Corps because Probst had considered these demands unreasonable and had simply ignored them!

This first hand-built prototype proved capable of taking everything which the Army testers could throw at it. So impressed was the Quartermaster Corps that it placed an order for a further 1,500 examples even before Bantam had completed the batch of 70 prototypes. These vehicles entered service – many with Allied forces rather than with the US Army – and were known as Bantam BRC-40s. Those initials stood for Bantam Reconniassance Car, 40bhp – which was the output of the Continental engine.

From a very early stage, however, the Quartermaster Corps had serious doubts about Bantam's ability to build the BRC-40 in the sort of volumes which would become

10

Willys Overland entered the contest rather late with their Quad design, of which just two were built.

necessary if the USA did go to war. So Bantam stood by helplessly while the blueprints of its design – which under the terms of the contract had now become military property – were handed over to Willys Overland and Ford. Both of these companies now expressed an interest in building prototypes at their own expense, and by November 1940 examples of the Ford Pygmy and Willys Quad were on test at Camp Holabird alongside the Bantams. Their basic design borrowed heavily from Bantam's pioneering work, but each incorporated a number of changes and individual features.

Most notably, each vehicle had its own maker's engine. The Ford had a modified tractor engine, which was the only four-cylinder type then in production at Dearborn, but this and the antiquated Model A transmission were major drawbacks which were retained when Ford built a revised model known as the GP (General Purpose) and submitted it for further trials. The Willys, however, had the latest version of its maker's Go-Devil side-valve four-cylinder which had been in production since 1926 and had most recently been updated by Chief Engineer Barney Roos for the Whippet saloon in 1938. With 63bhp, it offered much more power than either the Ford engine or the Continental type used in the Bantam, and it also came with a long pedigree of reliable service. Like the Bantam, the Quad was well over

11

Prototypes and the MA were earlier, but the vehicle recognized as the grandfather of the Jeep is the MB, built from 1941 to 1945.

the weight limit specified by the Quartermaster Corps, so when Willys Overland were given a contract to build 1,500 vehicles, they were told that the weight had to be cut down dramatically. It was – and the result was the Willys MA, which was actually considerably different from the Quad prototypes originally submitted for testing.

By this stage, the Quartermaster Corps' preference was already clear, and when the final tests were run between a Willys MA, a Ford GP and a Bantam BRC-40, no-one was very surprised to see the Willys come out as a clear winner. Bantam had to be content with second place, and Ford came a poor third. So on July 23, 1941, Willys Overland was awarded a contract to build 16,000 further revised models, which in due course became known as the MB. Nevertheless, the Quartermaster Corps was still worried about production capacity. So Bantam received a supplementary order to build just over 2,600 more BRC-40s (and subsequently bowed out of the Jeep programme),

and Ford swallowed its corporate pride and agreed to build the Willys MB under licence in its own factories. So, on November 10, 1941, the company was awarded an initial contract for a further 15,000 examples of what it called the Ford GPW (General Purpose Willys).

The Quartermaster Corps had got its new quarter-ton vehicle ready only just in time. On December 7, 1941 – less than six months after the date when Willys Overland was awarded that contract for 16,000 MB models – Japanese aircraft attacked the US Naval fleet at Pearl Harbour, in Honolulu, and the USA entered the Second World War. The Jeep went on to make a vital contribution to the Allied military effort all over the world and, in the words of George C Marshall, Chief of Staff during the war and later Secretary of State, 'The Jeep was the single most important contribution to the art of warfare.' It would later go on to make a major contribution to civilian life during peacetime, as well.

Willys MB and Ford GPW

The 1941 Willys MB became the definitive Jeep design, and even though it underwent a number of minor modifications (mainly to strengthen weak components) over the next few years, the Willys MB/Ford GPW proved a solid and enduring piece of machinery. It became a trusted companion of the GIs who fought in the Second World War, and it went with them all over the world as the war entered new theatres. It is certainly no exaggeration to say that the Jeep was the vehicle which brought mechanization to some areas of the world for the first time, and which thus opened up these areas to exports of motor vehicles when peace returned. Its rugged reliability, simple design and astonishing versatility made it into a military vehicle like no other before or since.

By the time the last Willys MB rolled off the assembly line on September 21, 1945 (the last Ford had been built earlier, on July 23), a total of 639,235 Jeeps had been built to the MB/GPW design. Of these, 361,339 had been made by Willys, and a further 277,896 by Ford. Nor was that the end of the design. In the USA, it went on to sire the Willys CJ-2A and a whole range of other civilian Jeeps, and outside the USA manufacturing licences were picked up by such as Mitsubishi in Japan and Hotchkiss in France. In fact, the Hotchkiss-built MB continued in production for the French Army until well into the 1950s, by which time Willys had moved on a long way from this original but still dependable design.

The basic concept of the MB can of course be traced back to Karl Probst's design for Bantam, but the production model actually drew on the Ford GP design as well as on Willys' own ideas. Most notably, the MB used the Ford's flat bonnet, which was altogether much more practical as a mobile table than the rounded design on the Willys MA. The first 25,808 Willys-built MBs (the majority built during 1941) also carried the Ford design of welded iron-slatted grille, although this proved prone to fractures in service and was replaced by the familiar pressed-steel grille panel. All the Ford-built GPWs, incidentally, had the pressed-steel panel from the time production started in January 1942.

The design of the MB was simplicity itself. The chassis

Bill Mauldin captured the affection which GIs had for their Jeeps in this immortal cartoon, showing a Cavalry Sergeant unable to look as he finishes off his wounded steed.

was a channel-section type with five cross-members, all of them also of channel-section except the front one, which was of tubular construction. (The Ford-built versions differed by having an inverted U-section front cross-member, but were otherwise to the Willys design.) The live

The Hotchkiss-built version of the MB was known as an M201. This preserved example carries the rear side reflector characteristic of the model.

axles were made by Spicer, and were sprung and located by semi-elliptic leaf springs made of aluminium alloy. Those on the front had eight leaves each, and those on the rear had nine. Split-rim combat wheels of 16-inch diameter carried tyres with a rugged, non-directional tread, and a spare wheel was mounted on the right-hand side of the rearward-facing body panel.

Up front was the unburstable four-cylinder Go-Devil engine, which drove through a Borg and Beck single-dry-plate clutch to a three-speed type T-84-J primary gearbox made by Warner. Like most designs of the time, this had no synchromesh on first gear. It had a floor-mounted gearshift, moved from its steering column location on the MA models because most military drivers were expected to be familiar with floor shifts from trucks. Drive was then taken to a two-speed transfer gearbox made by Spicer. This split the drive between front and rear axles, but the front axle normally freewheeled and was only engaged by using a lever alongside the gearshift, when the drive to the front wheels

provided extra traction for rough going. The higher of the two ratios in the transfer gearbox was engaged for normal road use, and permitted the Jeep a noisy and uncomfortable maximum speed of around 65mph. The lower ratio, selected by a third floor-mounted lever and available only when four-wheel drive was engaged, gave crawler gears to suit even tougher ground conditions.

The steel body tub was simple in the extreme, and had a two-pane windscreen which could be folded forwards onto the bonnet to lower the Jeep's profile or to facilitate air transport. The vehicle was open, but a degree of weather protection could be achieved by erecting tubular supports which hinged up from the tail of the tub and by fitting to them a canvas roof which was stowed under the front passenger seat when not in use. Even then, there was no side protection – and of course there were simple cutouts in the body sides instead of doors. Body and chassis were bolted together at 16 points, with rubber gaskets on early examples and fabric on later ones, when rubber became scarce. The two front seats had tubular frames, and the backrest of the rear bench right in the tail of the body could be folded down to increase cargo space. All seat covers were made of tough cotton duck, though padding material varied over the years.

Instrumentation was minimal, but gave the driver as much information as he needed to know about the health of his engine. Instruction plates screwed to the dashboard reminded him how to select four-wheel drive and low ratio, and made clear who had built the vehicle. Not that he needed to look there for confirmation, because Ford seemed obsessed with marking every component of the Jeeps they built with their own oval logo or with a stylized capital F. This obsession extended even to the tools in the vehicle's comprehensive toolkit! The first 25,000 Jeeps had also carried the name of their maker – Ford or Willys – embossed on the rear panel, but both companies had been asked by the US military to desist during 1941.

This, then, was the vehicle which really started it all. It proved itself in tough conditions of service, surviving with minimal maintenance and being distributed freely to Allied forces between its introduction in 1941 and the end of the war in 1945. Thousands were abandoned overseas when the American military forces withdrew at the end of the war because it was simply too expensive to bring them back home to the USA. Yet these abandoned vehicles, serviceable and otherwise, allowed the Jeep message to persist long beyond the end of hostilities.

The Seep
Jeeps rapidly proved their versatility on the battlefield, and military units soon adapted them to perform a huge variety of tasks which had probably never been imagined when the original specification was drawn up. Special variants appeared, too, among the most interesting being the 'Seep', a sea-going Jeep more properly known as a GP-A (General Purpose – Amphibious). This was designed by the Marmon-Herrington company in conjunction with the boat-builders Sparkman and Stephens, and was essentially a Ford GPW (never a Willys) with a boat-shaped steel hull. An initial order for 5,000 was placed in April 1942, but

The GP-A amphibian was never quite the success it's designers intended. All were built on Ford GPW chassis.

production was halted after 12,778 had been made. It appears that the Seep never quite lived up to expectations in the water.

The MC, alias M-38
The MB had set a trend for others to follow, and when it came time for the US military to replace some of its longer-serving examples in the late 1940s, Willys-Overland were ready to provide. By this stage, however, the Jeep had already moved some way beyond its purely military origins, and Willys Overland were enjoying success in the civilian market with derivatives of the original design. Among these was the CJ-3A (*see Chapter 2*), introduced in 1948, and it was on this that the design of the new military Jeep was based. Willys called the new model the Jeep MC, but it is more commonly known by its military code number M-38.

15

The MC or M-38 succeeded the MB and was manufactured between 1949 and 1952.

allowed for the running of additional electrical items such as two-way radios. The electrical system was waterproofed, of course, and the vehicle had a closed-loop breather system which was also designed to allow it to wade through deep water. This operated through a system of tubes which ran from the engine, gearbox, transfer box and fuel tank and ended up in the air cleaner. This was mounted high enough to remain clear of water at most times, and of course it could be connected to a snorkel-type breather for deep wading operations.

It was the M-38 Jeep which served the US military so well in Korea in the early 1950s, operating alongside remaining examples of the wartime MB. Many were also built under licence by Ford in Canada for the Canadian Armed Forces, and these were known as M-38CDN models. However, the M-38's life span was to be relatively short, because in 1951 Willys were asked once again to provide a new Jeep for military service. This one, the M-38A1, would become a sight almost as familiar as the MB had been in its heyday.

The MD, alias M-38A1

The third-generation military Jeep entered production in 1952, and was known to Willys as an MD model, but to the military as an M-38A1. It anticipated the design of the CJ-5 introduced in 1955 for the civilian market, which was later militarized itself for countries in receipt of American military aid. However, the only models to carry the M-38A1 designation were those built for the US Armed Forces. MDs were also built in Canada and in the Netherlands for local military use.

The M-38A1 followed the tried and tested military Jeep pattern, but it was a slightly larger vehicle than before, with an 81in wheelbase instead of the 80in of the earlier military models. The cargo bed was 3in longer, and the vehicle was capable of carrying a payload 100lb greater than the M-38 which preceded it. It was also visually distinctive, with a taller bonnet to accommodate its new engine, and downturned leading edges to the front wings, which had a more rounded profile than before. The windscreen was once again a two-pane type.

The M-38 entered production in 1949, and a total of 60,345 examples were built before production ceased in 1952. It was essentially a beefed-up CJ-3A, with that model's stronger rear axle and improved front axle shaft design, together with the latest version of the Go-Devil engine with a gear-driven camshaft instead of the earlier chain-driven design. Like the CJ-3A, it also had a single-pane windscreen in place of the MB's two-pane type, but in all visual respects it was quite clearly descended from the original wartime Jeep.

The M-38 nevertheless had a strengthened chassis-frame and body to withstand the unsympathetic treatment it was likely to get at the hands of GIs. In place of the 6-volt electrical system found on the CJ-3A and the original MB, it also had a military-standard 24-volt system, which

This M-38A1 preserved in the UK represents the military Jeep of the 1950s and 1960s. Also known as the MD, this was the last true military Jeep.

The new engine of the M-38A1 was simply a development of the old 134 cubic inch Go-Devil four-cylinder, with the same bore and stroke but a more efficient valvegear arrangement. The side exhaust valves remained, but the inlet valves were relocated in the cylinder head to give an F-head configuration. Thus modified, the engine would take on the name of Hurricane when introduced to the civilian market, which it was in the CJ-3B models in 1953. Gross power output was now up to 71bhp, still at 4,000rpm.

M-38A1 production continued in the USA until 1968, and more than 100,000 examples were built. However, this would be the last true military Jeep, for its replacement during the 1960s and 1970s was the Ford-designed M-151, also known as the MUTT. When a new generation of military vehicles was needed for the 1990s and beyond, the US Army turned to the much larger and more cumbersome

Humvee, built by AM General. By that time, Jeep no longer made a suitable vehicle.

The MDA or M-170
As its name suggests, the MDA was a derivative of the MD or M-38A1. It was built with an extra 20 inches in its wheelbase and was mostly used as a field ambulance or as a six-man troop carrier. Introduced in 1953, it pre-dated by two years the civilian CJ-6, which was essentially the same vehicle.

The MDA had the familiar Hurricane four-cylinder engine and was mechanically generally similar to the MD throughout. Its lengthened body tub was created by the insertion of an extra panel behind the door cutout, a crude but effective modification which was only too readily visible. Like the MD, the MDA was designed as an open vehicle, but was normally seen with soft top erect and, when

The long wheelbase of the MDA is clear in this picture of a preserved example in the UK.

equipped as an ambulance, with red-cross symbols on the sides of the canvas.

MDA production lasted until 1967, but it was not continuous. No MDAs were built between 1956 and 1961. In US military service, the MDA was known as an M-170.

Other military Jeeps

The MB, M-38 and M-38A1 were the foundations on which the military reputation of the Jeep was built, but they were far from being the only Jeeps to serve in military forces around the world. Militarized versions of the CJ-3A saw service in Belgium, Holland, Sweden and Switzerland among other places, and militarized CJ-3Bs (known as M-606 models when sold to recipients of the American Military Aid Programme) persisted into the 1960s. There were also militarized CJ-5s known as CJ-5M types, which were made available to MAP recipients as M-606A2 and

M-606A3 models.

Not to be forgotten, either, are licence-built versions of several Jeep models built in a variety of countries, and a few examples make clear how widely the military Jeep has been used. The militarized CJ-3B has been built by Mitsubishi in Japan (who fitted some versions with their own diesel engines), by Viasa (latterly Ebro) in Spain, who also offered a version with Perkins diesel power, and by Mahindra and Mahindra of Bombay in India. In Brazil, Willys built military versions of the CJ-5 during the 1960s and, after Willys Overland do Brasil and Ford do Brasil merged in 1969, these were renamed as the Ford U-50 Campaign. In the early 1980s, Keohwa began building Jeep designs at Seoul, in South Korea, for that country's military forces. These included versions of the CJ-5 and CJ-7, special long-wheelbase 0.75-ton trucks with CJ-style front panels, and 1.25-ton versions of the big J-series trucks.

CHAPTER 2

The classic flat-fenders

CJ-2A, CJ-3A and CJ-3B

Willys Overland started planning how to extend the Jeep's role into civilian life not long after the original MB had entered production. During 1942, work began on the sedan models which the company hoped to put into production when peace returned, and some consideration was also given at that time to an eventual civilian role for the Jeep. Then, at the end of 1943, Willys Overland's Vice-President, George C Ritter, was invited by a member of the US Congress to explain the way he saw the Jeep's civilian future.

Ritter argued that Willys would need to set up a proper dealer and servicing network before the Jeep could be marketed as a civilian vehicle. But he put forward a very clear vision of its value in agriculture. He saw it as a farm and ranch runabout which could double as a tractor or stationary power source, although he acknowledged that some redesign work would be necessary before it would adapt readily to this role. It needed the option of a power take-off, different gearing and a stronger clutch, and better cooling to cope with sustained low-gear work.

Before long the US Department of Agriculture picked up on these remarks and began to show a keen interest in the Jeep's future. Universities and other bodies began a series of experiments to examine the Jeep's peacetime potential, and the Agricultural Experiment Station of the State College of Washington even produced a 20-page booklet entitled *The Jeep as a Farm Truck-Tractor for the Post-War Period*. Further experiments determined the Jeep's suitability for tasks in forestry, ranching, mining and industry generally.

Willys had the redesigned civilian Jeep ready by the summer of 1945, and demonstrated it to the press on July 18 – just a fortnight before the expiry of the Government contract with Ford for manufacture of the GPW. The new model was known as a CJ-2A, the CJ obviously standing for Civilian Jeep and the 2 presumably reflecting the wartime MB's status as the first volume-produced Jeep. What the A suffix stood for never has been clear.

The basis of the simple but rugged MB remained unchanged, with the channel-section chassis, steel body tub, and 6-volt electrical system common to most cars of the time. However, Willys had made a number of important changes intended to give the vehicle a greater appeal in its new market. The 134ci side-valve Go-Devil engine could now be fitted with a governor to prevent accidental over-revving, such as might occur if wheelspin developed while towing farm implements across a ploughed field. A stronger clutch had been fitted, together with a Borg-Warner T-90 three-speed primary gearbox and ratios which differed from those of the MB's T-84-J type. The first CJ-2As (up to chassis number 13453) had a semi-floating Spicer Model 23-2 rear axle in place of the MB's fully-floating Model 25, and thereafter an even stronger Model 41-2 was specified.

More obvious than these mechanical improvements were that the load bed was now accessible through a removable hinged tailgate in the rear panel, and as a result of this the rear-mounted spare wheel had been relocated outside the load-bed on the right-hand side. The fuel filler was no longer under the driver's seat, but remotely mounted in the

The original CJ-2A of 1945 was easy to distinguish from its wartime MB ancestor, although the two were very alike in most respects. The side-mounted spare wheel would characterize CJs for the next three and a half decades.

The CJ-2A was conceived as an agricultural vehicle. Unlike the military MB, it had a tailgate, which has been removed in this picture. Note the rear lights: the proper lamp on the left is matched by a reflector on the right. The spare wheel is also missing here, but its mounting bracket can clearly be seen.

body side. There was a single tail lamp, positioned on the left-hand side, which was matched by a red reflector on the right. The headlamps were now 7in sealed-beam units, conventionally mounted on the surface of the grille panel rather than on hinged brackets behind it, and their surrounds were chromed. Early CJ-2As also had a column-mounted gearshift like that on the wartime MA, probably because Willys thought this would have greater appeal to buyers more used to driving cars than trucks.

Equally if not more important was that the CJ-2A was available with a vast quantity of dealer-installed options so that it could be equipped to suit the needs of individual buyers. Among the options were power take-offs, which could be fitted at the front, centre or rear of the vehicle. They enabled the engine to be used as a stationary power source to drive farm machinery or on-board equipment such as arc welders, generators or compressors. The idea of a stationary power source was not new, of course, and such power take-offs were commonly found on agricultural tractors. Indeed, Jeeps had been used as stationary power

This Colorado-registered CJ-2A has an aftermarket hard top and has been subtly updated.

sources during the war, when a drive-belt slung around a jacked-up wheel had enabled GIs in the field to drive a variety of machinery!

Willys tried very hard indeed to get the CJ-2A accepted as an agricultural vehicle, and their efforts paid handsome dividends. As part of its marketing effort, the company offered a whole range of agricultural implements which were designed to be towed behind the Jeep. These included ploughs, harrows, cultivators, mowers, graders, scrapers and terracers. From 1946, there was also a short-lived Fire Jeep, its fire pump mounted on an extended front bumper and driven from a power take-off, and its hoses stowed in lockers mounted on the rear body sides. Aftermarket manufacturers quickly got in on the act, too, with trailers designed to match the Jeep's wheeltracks and to share its wheels and tyres, a variety of steel hardtops – most of which gave the vehicle an ungainly or even sinister air – and other add-ons.

So when Willys advertised the CJ-2A as the Universal Jeep, their marketing slogan was well chosen. The vehicle did indeed have almost universal applicability, and could be used for a wide variety of jobs. However, it is important to recognize that the CJ-2A was always designed and sold strictly as a utility vehicle. The notion of a recreational Jeep simply did not exist at this stage in the marque's history, even though some more adventurous owners were probably already using their ex-military MBs and dealer-supplied CJ-2As to go where only horse or mule had ventured before. The last of 214,202 CJ-2A Jeeps left the assembly lines in Toledo in 1949, by which time the model had been superseded by a revised Jeep called the CJ-3A.

It is worth noting at this point that the Jeep had taken over completely at Willys Overland, and that it would be 1951 before the company resumed manufacture of the sedans which had been its bread and butter in the prewar years. The CJ-2A had been joined in 1946 by the first of a companion range of long-wheelbase Jeeps (see Chapter 6), and in 1947 Willys Overland posted annual sales of

This CJ-2A still works for its living, aided by some subtle updates such as the indicator/sidelamp units added to the front panel.

119,477 vehicles. This beat its previous record, established in 1929, and was far in excess of anything the company had managed to achieve in car production during the 1930s. The 1947 best-seller was the CJ-2A, which accounted for 65,078 of the vehicles which came off the assembly lines at Toledo.

The CJ-3A

It was no great surprise to find the successor to the CJ-2A bearing the CJ-3A designation, although what that A suffix stood for was still far from clear. The new model was introduced in 1948, and retained the classic appearance of earlier Jeeps with its flat fenders and 80in wheelbase. It brought several improvements, however, among them the single-pane windscreen glass, which enabled the CJ-3A to be distinguished from its predecessors at a glance. There

was also more legroom for those occupying the front seats, achieved at some expense to those on the still-optional rear bench.

Much more important, however, were the invisible modifications intended to improve the vehicle's durability. Thus, the camshaft of the 134ci Go-Devil engine was now driven by gears – noisier but more reliable than the chain-drive of the earlier engines. The rear axle had been upgraded once again, this time to a Spicer Model 44, and during production (at chassis number 37549) there was also an improved design of front axle shaft to counter a weakness at the hub end. The primary gearbox was still a T-90 three-speed with no synchromesh on first gear, and was operated by a floor shift, while the transfer gearbox still gave selectable four-wheel drive and the 6-volt electrics were retained.

The CJ-3A resembled the earlier CJ-2A very closely, but the single-pane windscreen was an instant recognition feature. This Dutch-registered example remains substantially original, and appears to be a late vehicle with the low-mounted wipers usually associated with the CJ-3B.

Production of the CJ-3A ceased at the Toledo plant in 1953, after 131,843 examples had been built. It had already been superseded by the further improved CJ-3B model, but it was not yet dead. In 1955, much of the CJ-3A was resurrected for the DJ-3A Dispatcher, and that model would continue in production until 1965.

The CJ-3B

The CJ-3B Jeep was announced in January 1953, and can now be seen as a transitional model between the classic flat-fender Jeep derived from the wartime MB and the newer models exemplified by the M-38A1 (introduced a year earlier) and CJ-5. Essentially, it was a re-engined CJ-3A, although it also boasted a number of other new features. The most obvious of these, to the casual observer, was that the windscreen wipers had been relocated from the top to the bottom of the single-pane windscreen.

Willys Overland had equipped the existing CJ-3A model with the new F-head version of the 134ci engine, which had already made its appearance in the M-38A1 military model and in the long-wheelbase Jeeps. This was known as the Hurricane engine, and boasted 75bhp as against the 63bhp of its predecessor. It was also taller than the old side-valve Go-Devil type as a result of its overhead inlet valves, and it would not fit under the bonnet of the CJ-3A. So the bonnet and grille panel were redesigned to accommodate the new engine, while the front wings remained unchanged from the previous design. The result was a rather oddly-proportioned vehicle, which nevertheless still looked like a traditional Jeep.

The CJ-3B was built not only in Toledo but also in a number of overseas countries where licence-manufacturing arrangements were made with local companies. Among the better-known CJ-3B clones were those made by Mitsubishi in Japan, where they were known as J3 models and could be bought with an optional diesel engine. Also interesting were the CJ-3 models made by Viasa in Spain, which combined the panelwork of the CJ-3B with the Go-Devil

The CJ-3B was characterized by its tall bonnet. This example, preserved in the UK, is actually a militarized M606 version, with wipers at the top of the screen.

engine of the CJ-3A.

Although the CJ-3B remained in production until 1968, its heyday was in 1953 and 1954, when it was the only CJ model Jeep in production. During 1954, the new CJ-5 model was announced, and once production of this one got into its stride during 1955, CJ-3B sales dropped to a third of their best levels. Sales went on declining, and towards the end of its life the CJ-3B was being built at a rate of just a few thousand each year. Nevertheless, the cumulative total of 155,494 examples built over its 16-year production life made it a model to be reckoned with in Jeep history.

CJ-4: the missing link
When Willys agreed licensing deals with overseas assembly and manufacturing plants for its Jeep products, the licensees were often given a fair degree of latitude to develop the basic design for local conditions. As already noted, Mitsubishi in Japan used their own diesel engine in some models, and a Perkins diesel engine was offered in Spanish-built Viasa and Ebro Jeeps. In India, where CJ-3B manufacture was licensed to Mahindra and Mahindra of Bombay, there was demand for a Jeep with more interior room, and an agreement was reached for the Indian company to develop a unique model to meet this demand.

The need was met quite simply by extending the wheelbase of the CJ-3B from 80 to 91in, and the resulting vehicle was christened a CJ-4. CJ-4 models were available with the standard CJ-3B drivetrain or with rear-wheel drive only, when there was no transfer box and a tubular front axle was fitted. They came with open bodywork or as enclosed Wagonette models.

The CJ-4 thus became the first extended-wheelbase CJ, pre-dating the Toledo factory's own CJ-6 derivative of the CJ-5 (*see Chapter 3*), and perhaps even pre-dating the MDA derivative of the M-38A1 military model (*see Chapter 1*). Unfortunately, it is not possible to obtain production figures for this variant, which was never built anywhere else in the world.

No it's not a Jeep. This CJ-3B lookalike is actually an Indian-built Mahindra from the early 1990s, and has a Peugeot diesel engine!

The Kaiser connection

Willys Overland certainly did not need any help to sell their CJ Jeeps in the early 1950s, but sales of the senior Jeeps (*see Chapter 6*) had begun to slide, and sales of the new car models announced in 1951 did not live up to expectations. The Korean War had led to a general slump in car sales, and Willys were too small to absorb losses for long. The company therefore responded favourably to an approach by the industrialist Henry J Kaiser during 1953.

Kaiser had made his fortune during the Second World War in the manufacture of Liberty ships, and after the war ended he had got together with former Willys Overland Chairman Joseph W Frazer to manufacture cars. Kaiser-Frazer cars sold well in the late 1940s but failed to make the

grade after the new decade opened, and Kaiser (always the senior partner) seized on Willys Overland as a good match for his own company. It had spare production capacity, which he could use to manufacture his own cars and so save costs, and its senior Jeeps badly needed a powerful six-cylinder engine like the one his company was already making. Moreover, sales of the CJs were strong enough to provide at least a temporary financial cushion.

So Kaiser Industries bought Willys Overland in April 1953 for $60 million. Kaiser-Willys set up its headquarters at the Willys plant in Toledo, sold the former Kaiser factory at Willow Run to General Motors, and began making Kaiser sedans alongside the Willys cars and Jeeps at Toledo. Just a year into the operation, however, it became quite clear that things were not going according to plan. Sales of the Kaiser and Willys sedans proved disappointing once again, so the company decided to cut its losses. Passenger car production stopped in 1955, and the tooling for the Willys Aero and Kaiser Manhattan models was sold to the Brazilian subsidiary of Willys, Willys do Brasil, which continued to make them until 1962.

Meanwhile, Kaiser left Jeep engineering well alone after donating its six-cylinder engine to the senior models. The company's biggest impact was perhaps in the way it encouraged Willys to pursue new markets for the Jeep, and there is no doubt that it played a big part in the expansion of Jeep assembly outside the USA. Over the 16 years when it owned the Jeep marque, Kaiser established manufacturing facilities in no fewer than 30 foreign countries, and marketed the Jeep in more than 150 countries worldwide.

On the right of this pair of CJ-5s, which are covered in the following chapter, is an early-1970s Renegade model, with grey accent striping. Note the A-frame on the bumper, allowing it to be towed to an off-road location by the owner's faster and more comfortable road car!

CHAPTER 3

At work and at play

CJ-5 and CJ-6

The classic shape and function of the CJ Jeeps was established in the late 1940s and early 1950s by the CJ-2A, CJ-3A and CJ-3B. These were workhorse vehicles, designed for all-terrain use and not intended for long-distance highway driving or for recreational off-road driving – although many owners discovered the fun to be had in tackling seemingly impossible terrain with a CJ for its own sake.

Even though the CJ-3B remained in production until 1968, on the US domestic market and in many overseas territories it had been superseded 13 years earlier by the CJ-5 model. This went on to become the longest-serving CJ Jeep of all time, with a production run which lasted for 28 years until 1983. Between 1955 and 1981, the CJ-5 was also accompanied by a long-wheelbase variant called the CJ-6. Yet long before its production ended, the CJ-5 had been superseded by the CJ-7, which was introduced in 1976 to spearhead Jeep's presence in the short-wheelbase 4x4 market.

The introduction of the CJ-7 was the logical outcome of important changes which had taken place in the CJs' market. The early CJs were uncompromisingly spartan vehicles, designed for a life of hard work and little else. However, the early 1960s saw the rise of the sport-utility market in the USA as 4x4 vehicles became popular for outdoor leisure activities. Kaiser Jeep responded to this change in a number of ways – the company's own 1963 Wagoneer being something of a pioneer of the new sport-

utility models – and one of these ways was to dress up the CJ-5 with luxury and convenience equipment of a type never before associated with the CJ range, and to offer it with the option of a large-capacity engine, which made it much more usable as a road vehicle for long-distance travel. This set the scene for models like the Jeepster Commando (*see Chapter 5*), and the new high-performance engine remained on the options list until it was replaced by engines offering even better road performance.

By the turn of the 1970s, it was quite clear that the CJ had found a new market. No longer primarily a workhorse vehicle, although still undoubtedly capable of sustained heavy-duty use, it had turned into a recreational 4x4. Special editions and option packages pandered to the new breed of CJ buyer, and when the CJ-7 was announced in 1976 there was no doubt that it had been designed for the recreational market rather than as a maid-of-all-work for commercial users.

The first CJ-5s, 1955-1971

The CJ-5 was introduced in October 1954, but much of its design dated from some years earlier because the new CJ was based on the MD or M-38A1, which had entered production for the military in 1952. The CJ-5 had the same 81in wheelbase as the MD, and the same more curvaceous front-end styling, 3in of extra length and 100lb of extra payload capacity in its rear load bed. Indeed, the very earliest CJ-5s also had the military-style split windscreen, although a single-pane type became standard during 1956.

The basis of the CJ-5 was traditional Jeep. There was a ladder-frame chassis with channel-section side-members and five cross-members, including a K-shaped reinforcing member at the rear. Suspension was by leaf springs all round, with beam-type live axles. The powertrain consisted of the 134ci Hurricane four-cylinder engine driving through a three-speed gearbox with a two-speed transfer gearbox offering selectable four-wheel drive. There were drum brakes and cam-and-lever steering. The basic vehicle came with only a driver's seat: all the others were optional at extra cost. A heater, too, was an extra-cost option.

Of course, there was a long list of optional extras available for the CJ-5, which enabled buyers to tailor the vehicle precisely to suit their individual needs. Power take-offs could be fitted at the front, at the rear, and in the

Both CJ-5 and CJ-6 were originally designed as working utility vehicles, and only later took on the recreational image so closely associated with them today. This publicity picture shows a CJ-5 on a construction site, where it primarily belonged in the 1960s, when the photo was taken.

There was no mistaking this hardtop-equipped CJ-5 as anything but a utility vehicle. The original factory-supplied metal top came with sliding doors.

The rugged outdoors nature of the CJ-5 is emphasised in this picture of an example splashing through water.

centre, and all of them took their drive from the transmission. Winches were available, normally fitted at the front of the vehicle and operated from the PTO. Agricultural implements and accessories could also be bought through Jeep dealers, and these included an angledozer, a terracing blade, a rotary broom, a rotary mower, a post-hole digger, a snow plough and a trencher. The load bed could be equipped with a crane and accessories to make the CJ-5 into a small breakdown truck. An uprated suspension, consisting of heavy-duty springs and dampers, was recommended with many of these options, and could also be bought independently of them. By 1965, a diesel engine (by Perkins in England), a Powr-Lok limited-slip front differential and freewheeling front hubs were also available.

Inevitably, the options list changed as time went on, but by 1960 the spotlight had fallen on those which would improve the CJ-5's road performance. The models of the late 1950s could not manage more than around 60mph flat-out, which was fine for local work, but uncomfortably slow if long distances had to be covered. So, from 1960, taller gearing of 4.27:1 was added to the options list as an alternative to the standard stump-pulling 5.38:1. This proved such a popular option that it had become standard by 1965, when the 5.38:1 ratio was relegated to the options list! Also new in 1960 was a four-speed transmission option, which paralleled the trend in the car industry towards transmissions with closer-spaced ratios which gave better acceleration response in the intermediate gears. Shortly afterwards, an overdrive for the three-speed gearbox was also made optional, this time as a dealer-installed accessory rather than a production-line fit.

As the 1960s opened, Kaiser-Jeep and others spotted the beginnings of a new market for four-wheel-drive vehicles. CJ Jeeps were being bought in small numbers for personal transport rather than as utilitarian workhorses, and although

The Universal Jeep was built in a number of overseas locations, but never in Britain. Nevertheless, in 1958 Kaiser-Willys approached Rover, makers of the rival Land Rover, with a proposal for Jeep manufacture in Britain. A single prototype, seen here, was built to test the viability of using Land Rover drivetrain components in a CJ-5 body and chassis.

the age of the sport-utility model had yet to dawn, there seemed to be a niche market for a light 4x4 which looked less like a utility model. Kaiser-Jeep tackled this first in 1961 with the Tuxedo Park edition of the CJ-5, chroming the bumpers, hood hinges and exterior mirror supports, and adding hubcaps to give a more car-like appearance. A full convertible top with side curtains was standard, as were padded upholstery and special hood badges. The Tuxedo Park cosmetic package remained optional in 1962 and 1963, and for 1964 became a model on its own with the name of Tuxedo Park Mark IV.

Sales brochures depicted it in the snow at a ski resort and at a yacht club, and there was no doubt that it was aimed at wealthy buyers – mostly as a second (or third or fourth) car. Bright paint colours added to its fashionable appeal. Obviously, its intended market was a limited one, and this was perhaps the main reason why sales never really took off, even when the Dauntless V6 option was introduced for 1965. For 1966, Jeep tried a slightly different tack with the

Prairie Gold limited-edition CJ-5, featuring similar chromework, special paint and soft top, and some interior upgrades. That did not set the market alight, either. Nevertheless, the Tuxedo Park remained available until the end of the 1968 model-year. By that time, the demands of the sport-utility market had become clearer, and Jeep had switched its marketing focus to the new Jeepster Commando models.

Meanwhile, the emphasis on developing the CJ-5 for road use had resulted in the 1965 introduction of a new engine option which represented perhaps the most important turning-point in the entire history of the CJ range. Even when the senior Jeeps (*see Chapter 6*) had been equipped with more powerful six-cylinder engines, neither Willys Overland nor Kaiser had seen any need to fit these engines into the CJs. At the time, the vast majority of CJ buyers were simply not interested in extra road performance and drivetrain refinement, but by the mid-1960s the position had changed irrevocably. As the sport-utility market opened up and the sedan market in the USA was dominated by the search for more power and speed, so Kaiser looked around for an engine which would give the CJ-5 some real road performance.

The latest Tornado overhead-camshaft six-cylinder introduced during 1962 in the Jeep Wagoneer would certainly have done the trick, but it was too large to fit into the engine bay of a CJ-5. Designed for a much bigger vehicle, it was also too heavy and would have upset the Jeep's handling. To develop an all-new engine for the CJ would have cost valuable time and money, and so Kaiser decided to see what might be available from other manufacturers.

As it happened, General Motors' Buick division wanted to sell the compact all-iron 60-degree V6 engine it had introduced in the early 1960s but now planned to replace with the bigger and more powerful V8s which were the fashion during the muscle-car era. The engine had first appeared in 1961 for 1962 models as a 198ci (3.2-litre) type, and with enlarged bores and a longer stroke had been reworked for a 1963 launch in 1964 models with a 225ci (3.7-litre) capacity and 155bhp instead of the 135bhp of the smaller-capacity original. Buick intended to keep it in production until mid-1967, but was happy to talk about a licensing deal with Kaiser and the eventual purchase of tooling and exclusive manufacturing rights. (As an aside, it is interesting to note that Buick also sold manufacturing rights to its 215ci all-alloy V8 at this time, the engine passing to Rover in Britain, who later turned it into the power unit of the Range Rover and other 4x4 vehicles from the Land Rover stable.)

It was already clear that the engine would fit into the CJ without difficulty because it had become a popular home conversion unit among Jeep enthusiasts. A deal was struck, and Kaiser got the new V6 engine into production as fast as they could. They changed almost nothing from the Buick original, although they did give the engine a new name: when fitted to the CJ Jeeps it was always known as a Dauntless V6. It first reached the showrooms during 1965, as an extra-cost alternative to the standard Hurricane four-cylinder. With 160bhp, it completely transformed the road

The CJ-5's interior was still resolutely spartan in 1970, when this publicity picture was taken.

performance of the CJ-5 and became a firm favourite with buyers who wanted a Jeep for anything other than ploughing a field or driving across a muddy construction site.

CJ-5s equipped with the Dauntless V6 came with the tough T-86AA three-speed transmission as standard, and from 1968 they had the all-synchromesh T-14 three-speed type. The transfer box always had a single-lever control. With the V6 engine also came taller 3.92:1 gearing than the four-cylinder models, with a 4.88:1 option to maximize torque and control for rock-crawling and other heavy-duty

The 1970 Renegade I package added a racing-type rollover bar, swingaway spare wheel carrier, heavy-duty oil pan, skid plate and electric ammeter and oil gauges, plus many cosmetic extras. The Dauntless V6 engine was standard.

rough-terrain work. The four-speed T-98A transmission was confined to the four-cylinder models, but of course V6 buyers could order an overdrive if they really needed higher gearing for more relaxed high-speed cruising. In such cases, the lower 4.88:1 axles were fitted. The V6 models also had more powerful brakes than the four-cylinders, with a larger swept area.

The V6 engine was always very much liked by CJ buyers in the second half of the 1960s, and it remained the only factory-installed alternative to the elderly Hurricane four-cylinder until 1971, when it was withdrawn as Jeep's new owner AMC introduced its own engines to the 4x4 range. The wheel came full circle, too. As the first oil crisis in 1973-74 led to a demand for smaller and more fuel-efficient engines and signalled an end to the muscle-car era, Buick bought back the V6 design and all its tooling from AMC.

The V6 then saw a further lease of life in large-bore 231ci form in 1975 and later-model Buick cars! By this time, however, it had been laden with emissions control equipment and produced a mere 110bhp . . .

By the end of the 1960s, Jeep had the experience of the Tuxedo Park behind it and was learning very rapidly from the presence on the market of the Dauntless V6 option and the Jeepster Commando (*see Chapter 5*). Perhaps the biggest lesson it learned was that luxury was only one element of a successful sport-utility vehicle; just as important was road performance. The developing market also had a strong youth orientation, and it was therefore price-sensitive. At the same time, competitive off-road events were becoming popular, so Jeep drew all this knowledge and experience together in a new CJ-5 model known as the 462.

The 462 was introduced as a limited-availability option package on the CJ-5 in late 1969, and it represented the first sporty CJ. In theory, it was ready for competition as it came from the showroom, although most buyers who were serious about using it competitively would surely have thrown away the ridiculous stainless steel wheel covers (which differed from those on the Tuxedo Park limited edition) and the tow hitch. Otherwise, the 462 package consisted of a reinforced chassis-frame equipped with heavy-duty suspension, a skid plate and a limited-slip differential in the rear axle. Tyres were fashionable red-stripe Polyglass tubeless types. The Dauntless V6 was the only engine option and came with a reinforced oil pan. The body came with a padded safety rail on the dash, a rollover bar and safety harnesses front and rear, while the spare wheel had been moved from its side-mounted position to a military-style swingaway carrier on the rear panel. Additional instrumentation in the shape of an oil gauge and ammeter completed the picture.

The 462 was used as the basis of another limited-volume sporty model in 1970. This was called the Renegade I, and was much more obviously designed to create an image for its buyers. Like the 462, the Renegade I had a boxed frame and heavy-duty suspension, plus the Dauntless V6. It had a rollover bar, padded safety rail, the rear-mounted swingaway spare wheel carrier and extra gauges. For visual appeal, there were garish side decals and striped upholstery (both fashionable on the sporty muscle cars of the day), plus – once again – bright wheel covers.

Both the 462 and the Renegade I exploited the new recreational 4x4 market, and a fascinating additional accessory introduced in 1969 for V6 models only took the theme in another direction. This was known as the Jeep Camper, and it consisted of a two-wheeled camper which attached to the back of a CJ-5 and extended over its cab roof as far forwards as the windscreen. Inside, the camper unit was extremely well-equipped, with a kitchen, toilet, stowage cabinets and sleeping room for four – the latter an unnecessary luxury, perhaps, as no more than three could travel in the Jeep's cab! Once a camp site had been found, according to the sales brochure, 'the camper is easily detached from the 'Jeep' Universal. And

that means in a few short minutes you've got a vacation home that doesn't have to move until you say the word. Your 'Jeep' Universal is free for more adventure. More hillsides to climb. Or even a short trip back to the country store.'

It seemed like an excellent idea, but somehow the Jeep Camper never sold very well. American buyers preferred their full-sized motorhomes, and the Camper became an unloved and forgotten variant.

JEEP AND AMC

By the end of the 1960s, Kaiser's investment in Jeep was paying dividends. Profits were healthy, sales were up, and the Jeep Corporation's future looked good. However, the Kaiser Industries Corporation planned to consolidate its

A CJ-5 is seen here in use by highway police in the USA. It is equipped with an all-weather top, winch, heavy-duty push bumper and freewheeling front hubs.

The CJ-5 wheelbase was stretched by 3 inches to accommodate the long AMC six-cylinder engines for 1972. Note the thin-band whitewall tyres and the rollover bar on this model.

activities, and so decided to put Jeep up for sale.

American Motors Corporation (AMC) – already supplying engines to Jeep under contract – was the ideal buyer. It was the last of the big independent US motor manufacturers, but it had no trucks or four-wheel-drives to compete with the Big Three companies' offerings in those areas. Jeep did, so the deal was agreed for around $75 million.

One of AMC's first acts was to hive off military vehicle production into a separate division called AM General. While the Jeep marque continued to thrive, AMC's own cars did not. As funds became short, AM General was sold off; but by the end of the 1970s the industry recession was hitting AMC hard. So in 1980 it sold 46.4% of its shares to the French Renault company. Even this was not the long-term answer. By 1986, AMC was in the red again, and Renault decided to pull out. Jeep changed hands again in 1987 for approximately $2 billion. The buyer this time was the Chrysler Corporation.

The CJ-5 under AMC

When American Motors bought the Jeep Corporation from Kaiser-Willys in 1970, the American motor industry was already under immense pressure from new legislation which demanded cleaner exhausts and more safety features in its products. It was extremely costly to redevelop existing engines to meet the exhaust emissions regulations, which the Government had already warned would get tighter as the decade wore on, and the effect of the emissions controls was to stifle engine power. There was no point in developing the old Hurricane four-cylinder engine to meet the new regulations as it was grossly underpowered already.

The cheapest option was for AMC to use its own car engines in the Jeep range, as these were already being developed to meet the latest regulations and had plenty of the power that the Jeep needed. Of these, the entry-level 232ci (3.8-litre) six-cylinder had started life in the 1964 Rambler Typhoon, while the 258ci (4.2-litre) was a long-

The spare wheel was still carried on the side of the CJ-5 when AMC took over, and would remain there for a few more years.

This 1976 CJ-5 carries the sporty Renegade package. Note also the Levi's decal above the Jeep name, just ahead of the door. This indicates that the vehicle has the weatherproof vinyl soft-top and upholstery option.

stroke development of it, new for the 1971 season. Both were too long to fit into the existing CJ-5 engine bay, but AMC reasoned that it was still a better solution to stretch the Jeep than to try to make either the Hurricane four-cylinder or the Dauntless V6 meet forthcoming emissions regulations. The 232 engine offered 100bhp as certificated for the 1972 season – usefully more than the Hurricane's 70bhp and therefore in line with customer demands for more power – and the 258 promised 110bhp. Both had the ample reserves of torque at low engine speeds which are needed in an off-road vehicle. So that the absence of the Dauntless V6 would not be felt too keenly, AMC decided to offer its own 304ci (5-litre) V8 as the top performance option in the CJ-5. With 150bhp, it was more than powerful enough for the job. However, fuel economy – not really an issue at this stage – was nowhere near as good as on earlier CJs, and so AMC fitted all models with a bigger fuel tank, which held 16.5 gallons instead of the 14 gallons of earlier types.

So, beginning with the 1972 models, the CJ-5 came with

an 84in wheelbase and a choice of three engines instead of the two available earlier. However, the AMC revamp of the by now elderly CJ amounted to very much more than that. The extra weight of the new engines had been matched by stronger front springs, and the steering boasted a lower ratio than before to ease low-speed manoeuvring. In fact, the whole steering system was new, being a GM Saginaw recirculating-ball type in place of the traditional CJ cam-and-lever system; power assistance was also available with all three engines.

The extra grunt of the three new AMC engines had made a number of driveline upgrades necessary. Thus, the clutch on all three CJ-5 models was increased in diameter to 10.5in from the earlier 9.25in. Standard transmission was a three-speed all-synchromesh type, and this was the only choice for the V8 models, but buyers of the two sixes could order a heavy-duty four-speed gearbox with no synchromesh on first gear. A floor shift was made standard on all models, and in all cases the drive was taken through a Dana Model 20 transfer box giving selectable four-wheel drive. Low ratio was raised to 2.03:1 from the 2.45:1 of the Dana Model 18 in earlier CJ-5s to protect the rest of the driveline from the effects of the new engines' massive torque, although climbing ability was unaffected by the change. A welcome additional benefit was a longer control lever for the transfer gearbox.

Overall gearing was now a high 3.73:1, with a low 4.27:1 ratio optional. Both front and rear axles had also been uprated. At the rear, the new axle was capable of dealing with 3,000lb as against the 2,500lb of the earlier type, while at the front a Dana Model 30 replaced the earlier Model 27. This brought with it a slightly wider track, but its open-ended balljoint steering arrangement allowed the wheels to turn at a greater angle and thus reduced the CJ-5's turning circle by some 6ft – a quite astonishing achievement for a vehicle with greater length and wheel track than the one it replaced! The brakes had also been uprated, and all the AMC-engined models had 11in drums instead of the 10in type on earlier CJ-5s. They also had a foot-operated parking brake instead of the central handbrake lever traditional to the CJs, and power assistance was an option – though only

with the 304 V8 engine.

The side-mounted spare wheel had always been an embarrassment in certain types of off-road driving, so AMC introduced an optional fixed mounting on the CJ-5's rear panel as an alternative – which brought with it a solid rear panel instead of the traditional drop-down tailgate. As before, the driver's seat was the only standard seating in the vehicle, all the others being extra-cost options. A front bench seat with a one-third/two-thirds split was a new offering, and all seats, front and rear, were of a new and more comfortable design with foam padding. As on the earlier 462 and Renegade I models from Kaiser, an auxiliary instrument package consisting of ammeter and oil pressure gauge could be had. Lastly, it said something about the new breed of CJ buyers that AMC felt it important to offer an ashtray as an optional extra: in earlier times, CJ owners had simply used the great outdoors!

AMC continued to strengthen the CJ range for 1973, introducing a mechanical clutch linkage in place of the troublesome cable type, which dated back to the wartime MB. The 1973 CJ-5 also had a redesigned dashboard with soft-feel knobs, international code symbols, and better illumination for the dials, which now sported orange needles. There was also a two-speed wiper motor, with a linked washer cycle. For 1974, CJ-5s gained improved body-to-chassis mounts, new brakes with proportioning valves in the hydraulic lines, and a more powerful heater. As an option, they could also be fitted with energy-absorbing bumpers, which that year became mandatory on new cars sold in the USA. For the time being, the CJs were classified as trucks and were therefore exempted from this regulation, but AMC clearly intended to be prepared in case of a change in the legislation. The energy-absorbing bumpers never did prove popular on CJ-5s, however.

The main focus of CJ development now switched to the new CJ-7 models, and the 1977-model CJ-5s introduced in autumn 1976 incorporated several changes inspired by the new CJ. First off was the fully-boxed chassis-frame, with flared rear side-members to improve rear spring location and a wheelbase reduced in consequence by half an inch to 83.5in. The 1977 CJ-5s also had the CJ-7's Dana Model 30

Unmistakable badging on a CJ-5. The plate underneath shows that this was imported in the early 1970s by the UK specialists, Howes.

front axle and smaller-diameter steering wheel, and their Spicer Model 44 rear axles – traditional to the CJ line since the beginning – were replaced by AMC's own Model 20 axle. Disc front brakes with power assistance became optional that year, and the optional four-speed heavy-duty transmission was commonized with its counterpart on other Jeep models, acquiring lower intermediate gears and an ultra-low 6.32:1 first. The rear of the body tub was strengthened, and new options included a centre console and – of all things in a CJ-5 – air conditioning.

Mechanical changes over the next couple of years were dictated to a large extent by exhaust emissions regulations. Catalytic converters had been obligatory in California since 1976, and they were fitted to all 1978-model CJ Jeeps to simplify production. It also looked good, as Federal regulations did not demand catalytic converters until a year later. For 1979, however, AMC had other plans. They dropped the 232ci in-line six altogether, leaving the 258ci engine as the entry-level type and fitting it with a two-barrel carburettor to improve power and torque slightly. The 304

A right-hand-drive CJ-5? Yes – one imported and converted by the UK specialists Howes in the early 1970s.

V8 thus became the only optional engine for 1979, switching from a four-barrel carburettor to a two-barrel type and losing power in the process. This was the only way AMC could make it meet the latest emissions controls. AMC did offer some compensation, though, by offering the rugged T-18 transmission as an option on V8 models in place of the standard T-15 type.

The problem with exhaust emissions controls was that they not only sapped engine power, but also tended to increase fuel consumption. Just as the full effects of this were being felt on the 1979-model Jeeps, the world was plunged into a second oil crisis by events in the Middle East. Petrol prices shot up, and the public (followed in due course by the US Congress) began to demand vehicles with better fuel economy. AMC had no new and more economical engines in the pipeline, so the company swiftly did a deal with the Pontiac division of General Motors and bought in that company's 151ci (2.5-litre) four-cylinder pushrod OHV engine, a reliable and durable lightweight unit first seen in 1977-model sub-compact sedans from the GM company. It appeared in 1980-model AMC sedans and in 1980-model CJ-5 Jeeps (and would remain available in Pontiac models throughout the 1980s). With just 86bhp, it was never going to offer the performance of the big AMC engines, but Jeep attempted to improve its appeal by giving it the Hurricane name used on the legendary four-cylinder last seen in Jeeps for 1971. Few people were impressed by this, however, and the engine has always been more commonly known by its Pontiac name of Iron Duke.

Allied to tall 3.54:1 gearing, the new four-cylinder engine nevertheless did bring fuel economy of a different order to that offered by the six- and eight-cylinder engines. With it, and with the optional 258ci six and 304ci V8 engines as well, came a new close-ratio Warner T-5 four-speed transmission in a lightweight aluminium alloy casing. While this was not as strong as the transmission it replaced, it did come with a new Dana 300 transfer box which brought a 2.6:1 low ratio (in place of the earlier 2.03:1) to offset the effects of the higher overall gearing. Locking front hubs and a new hardtop with metal doors were also new for 1980. Then, for 1981, more weight was saved through a lightweight version of the 258ci six-cylinder engine, which lost 90lb through the use of aluminium and plastic. That year also saw axle ratios raised yet again, to an astonishing 2.73:1 for both the four-cylinder and six-cylinder CJ-5s.

From the beginning, AMC had set about marketing the CJ-5 more imaginatively, with a whole series of special editions and option packages which set the tone for Jeep marketing into the 1990s. Early 1971 brought the Renegade II, of which just 600 were made, all distinguished by striking green, orange or yellow paint with grey accent stripes. The Renegade option package remained available for 1972 and 1973, when it was always accompanied by the 304 V8 engine, then for 1974 the CJ-5 Renegade became a regular production model. It would remain the sporty CJ-5 until production ended in 1983.

Meanwhile, there had been a Super Jeep option for 1973, essentially a dressed-up six-cylinder CJ-5. For 1975, a deal with the jeans manufacturer brought a Levi's upholstery and soft-top option – accompanied by Levi's decals on the bodywork – although in fact this was a weather-resistant vinyl in blue or tan and not the denim its name suggested. Things then went quiet for a while on the CJ-5 front, in order not to steal any thunder from the new CJ-7 model introduced during 1976, but by mid-1978 AMC were ready to offer another two special packages.

For the 1979 season only there was a 25th Anniversary package with silver metallic paint, silver accent stripes, a black soft-top, black bucket seats and a commemorative dash plaque. The second package was more enduring, and was known as the Golden Eagle. This had a huge spread-eagle decal on the hood panel, accent stripes on the body sides and grille, gold-coloured wheels and wide all-terrain tyres, plus black fender extensions. The soft-top was made of tan Levi's material, and bucket front seats, a rev-counter and a rollover bar were standard. It proved popular, too: 2,000 had been planned, but sales in that first year justified production of 2,200 examples. Meanwhile, the success of the CJ-7 had made clear that most CJ customers wanted comfort and convenience features above all else, and so these were stressed in the new Laredo package introduced on 1980 models. This again proved an enduring option and, like the Renegade, remained available until the end of CJ-5 production.

Regardless of what dyed-in-the-wool Jeep enthusiasts may have thought, AMC had certainly understood the market. The arrival of the CJ-7 and the upgrading of the CJ-5 led to a sales explosion, and in June 1978 these models were responsible for a substantial proportion of the 14,000 Jeeps of all kinds sold that month – a new record for the marque. Production capacity at the Toledo factory had already been expanded 15 times since AMC had taken over, and during 1978 AMC stopped production of cars at its Canadian factory in Brampton, Ontario, and turned it over to CJ manufacture. This in turn freed up more space at Toledo for assembly of the strong-selling J-series trucks.

This euphoria was to be short-lived, however, and CJ-5 sales started to drop again after 1979. One reason was the industry-wide recession induced by the second fuel crisis that year. Then, on December 21, 1980, the CBS TV programme *60 Minutes* dealt a blow to sales when it

A right-hand-drive CJ-6, almost certainly converted by the British importers in the mid-1970s. Despite their more overtly utilitarian nature, CJ-6s also found favour with recreational buyers.

demonstrated how easily a CJ-5 could be made to roll over. It must be said that anyone who expected the tall and narrow vehicle to behave like a low-slung sports car under hard cornering perhaps needed an injection of common sense. Nevertheless, that was the way the American consumer industry was going by the early 1980s, and even though an investigation by the National Highway Traffic Safety Administration deduced that there was no safety defect in the design of the CJ Jeeps, the damage had already been done.

This was just the first nail in the CJ-5's coffin, however. Sales stumbled badly a year later when tougher emissions regulations in California meant that the 304 V8 had to be withdrawn from one of its biggest markets. By 1982, it had also disappeared from the other 49 states of America. Despite the arrival of the Renault 2.1-litre diesel as an export option during 1982 (*see Chapter 4*), AMC decided that the CJ-5 was no longer sustainable. In any case, the newer CJ-7 more accurately reflected customer tastes in the 1980s. There were also bigger fish to fry, and AMC did not want to be the centre of bad publicity just before the launch

This British-registered CJ-5 Renegade dates from the early 1980s.

This CJ-6 has been heavily personalized by its British owner, with a suspension lift kit, big wheels and tyres and a whole collection of other features.

of the new XJ Cherokee range. So in 1983 the CJ-5 was dropped. A total of 603,303 had been built, together with 7,394 CJ-5As, to make these by far the best-selling variant of the whole CJ line.

The CJ-6 and CJ-6A

One of the biggest problems with the CJ line of Jeeps was a lack of interior space. It was not so much a question of load space as legroom for those in the rear, where the rear bench seat was really little more than a token – and an extra-cost one at that! So plans were drawn up to offer long-wheelbase editions of the CJ models, and the first was the CJ-4, which was built only in India for the local market.

The CJ-4 was a derivative of the CJ-3B, with a wheelbase of 92in. However, this still did not make the vehicle long

enough to meet the military's requirement for a field ambulance, and so the MDA was developed with 101 inches between axle centres. This vehicle (*see Chapter 1*) was introduced in 1953, and it was probably the Kaiser management which decreed that it should be used as the pattern for a long-wheelbase civilian Jeep, which reached the market in 1955 as the CJ-6 model.

Like the military MDA, the CJ-6 had its 20 inches of extra length inserted ahead of the rear axle and behind the front seats, and they were clearly visible on the outside of the body tub, where the original wheelarch cutout remained visible at the front of an additional panel specially shaped to fit it. In most other respects, however, the CJ-6 was the same as the CJ-5 on which it was based. The CJ-6s always had the same drivetrain options, and when AMC stretched the wheelbase of the CJ-5 to accommodate its longer six-cylinder engines, the CJ-6s gained the same 3in of sheet metal and chassis-frame to end up with a wheelbase of 104in. By the same token, the redesigned chassis-frames which came in for 1977 took the wheelbase of the CJ-6 back down to 103.5in.

Customers for the CJ-6 were very largely construction companies and other commercial concerns who needed the ruggedness and four-wheel drive but were less concerned about ultimate off-road agility. Optional equipment such as a backhoe and a post-hole digger was available for the CJ-6 in exactly the same way as for the CJ-5. Yet there were also passenger-carrying variants on offer such as a Tuxedo Park Mark IV edition of the CJ-6 in the USA in the mid-1960s. In addition, the Station Wagon body available in some export markets (*eg* Australia, where CJ-6 models were assembled in Brisbane in the early 1960s) was clearly designed to make the vehicle into a passenger-carrier rather than a pure commercial.

By 1975, it was clear to AMC that the real money was to be made in sales of recreational 4x4s rather than in the sales of specialist commercial vehicles, so production of the CJ-6 stopped at the Toledo factory. Nevertheless, overseas assembly of CJ-6s lasted for another five years until 1981, when the CJ-7-derived Scrambler was introduced.

CHAPTER 4

The recreational Jeep

CJ-7, CJ-8, Wrangler YJ and Wrangler TJ

When Jeep adapted the utility CJ-5 models to the demands of the recreational sport-utility market in the 1960s, it did so successfully enough for the models to remain available until the early 1980s. Yet, with the spotlight firmly on recreational 4x4s, and the small utility market falling to rugged pick-ups from a variety of manufacturers, AMC knew that the future would demand a very different kind of vehicle. The CJ-5 with its military-utility pedigree was not that vehicle. What was wanted was a CJ Jeep designed specifically for the recreational market.

So towards the middle of the 1970s, AMC set to work on the design of the very first recreational CJ, which would reach the market in October 1975 as a 1976 model called the CJ-7. The company recognized how important it was not to reject the heritage of the CJ line, however, and so one of the major design criteria was that the new recreational CJ should be recognizable as a descendant of its forebears.

Meanwhile, market research made clear that recreational CJ buyers wanted a number of features which were not available on the CJ-5. For a start, they wanted more interior room, but not as much as was offered by the rather cumbersome long-wheelbase CJ-6. They also wanted simpler transmission controls, among them an automatic transmission and a permanent four-wheel drive option which would leave the only transfer lever control as the one which switched from high to low ratio. They wanted a better ride and more comfort, easier access to and exit from the vehicle, and improved instrumentation. It is all too easy to see these requests as a desire to soften the essence of the

CJ and to turn it into some kind of luxury boulevard cruiser, but the truth is that what the buyers wanted was more convenience in the vehicle without any loss of its practicality. So it was this which AMC set about addressing.

The obvious way of incorporating all these new features into the CJ was to lengthen its wheelbase. This would bring more interior room and a better on-road ride, and the extra length would also make room for a General Motors Turbo-Hydramatic 400 automatic transmission of the type available in the big Wagoneer and Cherokee models for many years. So a wheelbase size of 93.4in was chosen as the minimum necessary to fit around this package. This made the new CJ-7 considerably bigger than any earlier US-built standard-wheelbase CJ, and actually bigger than the first (CJ-4) long-wheelbase model built in India! However, the CJ-7 fitted neatly between the CJ-5 and the much bigger Wagoneer and Cherokee models, so AMC was able to promote it as an intermediate-wheelbase model when it first reached the market.

If this new model were to be subjected to the punishment which CJ-5 models were taking from off-road driving enthusiasts, its longer wheelbase would clearly make the chassis more prone to stress fractures. Determined to avoid that, the design engineers therefore went for a modified frame with boxed-in side-members to give additional strength. At the same time, these side-members were splayed outwards over the rear axle to allow the rear spring mountings to be repositioned nearer the sides of the vehicle for additional roll resistance.

The CJ-7 was new in August 1975 as a 1976 model. The example shown here has the optional plastics composite hardtop and the full-depth metal doors to go with it. The bright wheel covers were also an option.

Details of the sporty Renegade package differed from year to year. This is a 1976 model.

Front-end roll was less of a problem, but the Jeep designers made an anti-roll bar optional and, to minimize kickback through the tighter new recirculating-ball steering system when the CJ-7 was being driven on rough ground, they also offered a hydraulic steering damper as an option. Power-assisted steering was yet another option, and made the whole business of driving a CJ-7 much less like driving a truck and more like driving a car. As for the brakes, there were drums on all four wheels on the first season's CJ-7s, but on 1977 models those on the front wheels were replaced by 11.75in diameter discs. When backed up by power assistance, these gave reassuring stopping power, which was particularly welcome with the bigger engine options.

Engine options were unchanged from those in the CJ-5 of the time, with the 232ci six being the entry-level motor and the 258ci six and 304ci V8 being available at extra cost. Over the years, these two larger engines were modified in exactly the same way as for CJ-5 models. However, with the transmission options, the CJ-7 introduced a whole new set of complications. Standard was a new heavier-duty three-speed manual type, harnessed to a Dana Model 20 two-speed transfer box with a 2.03:1 low ratio. Optional, as on the CJ-5, was a four-speed with an ultra-low first gear, and of course there was also the Turbo-Hydramatic 400 three-speed automatic option. This latter came with Warner's new Quadra-Trac permanent four-wheel-drive transfer gearbox, which split the drive between front and rear axles but did not offer a low-ratio gearset. Low range was available only by adding an optional reduction unit to the rear of the automatic gearbox, when a 2.57:1 step-down ratio was available. In all cases, and with all engines, the standard final-drive ratio was a high 3.54:1 to give good highway cruising speeds; off-road driving enthusiasts, however, tended to prefer the low 4.09:1 axle option. With both manual transmissions, but not with the automatic, a Powr-Lok limited-slip rear differential was also available as an extra-cost option.

The CJ-7 also had a number of new body features.

Perhaps most important was the new optional polycarbonate hardtop, available in black or white, which turned the vehicle into a compact station wagon. This came with metal doors incorporating wind-up windows – another first on a CJ – and with a metal tailgate hinged from the roof and terminating at waist level. The door cutouts in the body tub had straighter rear edges than on earlier models, to improve access, and the windscreen was very slightly more raked. Detail improvements also made their own contributions, such as the relocation of the wiper motor behind the windscreen and the consequent elimination of the unsightly bulging metal cover at the base of the screen on the left-hand side.

The instrument layout on the CJ-7 was much clearer and more car-like than on previous CJs, although the dials were all located together in the centre of the dashboard in order to simplify assembly of versions with both left-hand and right-hand drive. An energy-absorbing (collapsible) safety steering column was also standard, even though this was not yet mandatory under US regulations, and it came with a

The Laredo package arrived for 1980 and brought extra luxury items as well as unique cosmetic features.

Right at the top of the CJ-7 tree for 1982 was the CJ-7 Limited, the most comprehensively equipped CJ to that date. It was a good looker, too.

new steering wheel of smaller diameter to improve the car-like feel of the controls. For extra cost, buyers could have a steering column which adjusted to six different positions. Full carpeting was not something CJ owners had been used to, while factory-fitted air conditioning, a cruise control, a centre console and a stereo radio were available as options for the first time.

AMC exploited the special-edition theme for all it was worth with the CJ-7, beginning with a sporty Renegade package. This was easily recognized by special decals on the sides of the hood, blue or tan seat trim in denim-look vinyl, and white-finished multi-spoke wheels with 8in rims. There was a swingaway spare wheel carrier at the rear, while the interior featured a soft-feel sports steering wheel, a grab bar, cigar lighter and rear seat as standard. The success of this concept led to the Golden Eagle limited edition of 1978-79,

which paralleled the package of the same name available on the contemporary CJ-5. Special paint, the spread-eagle hood decal, accent striping, gold-painted wheels and wide tyres with black fender extensions all made this a distinctive and sought-after package.

The focus of the special editions of the 1980s was different, however. The Laredo was the first to arrive, on 1980 models, and it was unashamedly a luxury package. Laredo models had an abundance of chrome, which decorated wheels, grille panel, mirrors and bumpers, and they had more luxurious interiors – although air conditioning, cruise control and the stereo radio were still extra-cost options. Then April 1982 brought the CJ-7 Limited, which went so far as to feature the option of leather upholstery. It also had softer suspension as standard, an upholstered removable hardtop, a padded rollover bar, spoked wheels, a chromed front bumper, body stripes, power brakes and steering, and a stereo radio. Despite its enthusiastic acceptance, the Limited proved to be exactly what its name promised, and went out of production for 1984. Meanwhile, 1982 had also seen 2,500 examples of a 30th Anniversary Commemorative Edition CJ-7, which celebrated three decades of the annual Jeep enthusiasts' gathering, the Jeepers' Jamboree. These had special Jamboree decals, a Jamboree spare wheel cover, and a number of other unique details.

The mechanical specification of the CJ-7 also underwent some important changes in the 1980s. The 232ci six-cylinder engine was dropped in favour of Pontiac's Iron Duke 151ci four-cylinder in 1980 as concerns about fuel economy became a critical factor in car purchase after the 1979 oil crisis. The Quadra-Trac transfer box was no longer offered, either, as its permanent four-wheel drive was considered to use more fuel than the selectable type, and the thirsty 304ci V8 was dropped in 1981 to leave only the four-cylinder and the 258ci six on offer. From 1980, lightweight transmission components were used, as on the CJ-5, and the automatic transmission was no longer a Hydramatic but rather a Chrysler Torque-Flite (though a type 999 instead of the 727 used in the senior Jeeps). From the spring of 1982, a Warner SR4 all-synchromesh four-speed manual transmission became standard equipment while the new Borg-Warner T-5 five-speed was made optional. Then, from 1984, the entry-level four-cylinder engine was replaced by a new 150ci AMC-designed four-cylinder, which was essentially two-thirds of the existing six-cylinder type.

There was little doubt in the minds of buyers that AMC had emasculated the CJ-7 in its attempts to satisfy customer concerns and Government legislation about fuel economy. Sales had peaked in 1979, and never again reached the same levels, although 1984 and 1985 did see a revival of the CJ-7's fortunes, sparked mainly by the withdrawal of the CJ-5 during 1983. Yet when AMC announced in November 1985 that production of the CJ line would end early in 1986, there was a public outcry. The CJ Jeeps had come to represent the American ideal of individual freedom, and for many owners had become an icon. Even though the model which replaced them offered many of the CJs' characteristics, it was simply too sophisticated to satisfy enthusiasts used to the jolty, noisy, wind-in-the-hair character of the recreational CJs.

Like its predecessors, the CJ-7 was built under licence or assembled from American-made kits in a number of overseas locations. Some of these overseas assembly operations equipped the vehicles specially to suit local market conditions, and thus in Australia from 1981, the CJ-7 could be bought with a 145ci (2.4-litre) Japanese-built Isuzu four-cylinder diesel engine of 65bhp. Meanwhile, the French Renault company had taken a major (46%) stake in AMC during 1979, partly in order to gain a foothold for its own cars in the US market, and one result was that Renault dealers in France began to distribute Jeep products. So, from November 1982, the CJ-7 could be bought in France with the same 127ci (2.1-litre) four-cylinder Renault diesel engine introduced in the CJ-5, which came only with the five-speed gearbox. The Renault engines were shipped to Toledo for installation, and then the completed vehicles were shipped back to France for sale there.

The CJ-8 Scrambler
The 1980s were not all bad news for the CJ line, however,

The CJ-7 always had a cult appeal in Europe. This is a French-registered example.

because March 1981 brought a new long-wheelbase model based on the CJ-7. In terms of Jeep production, it replaced the CJ-6, which went out of production in 1981, even though it had not been sold on the US domestic market for five years. However, the new long-wheelbase model was not at all the same kind of vehicle as the CJ-6 and was not really a replacement for it. The CJ-6 had been simply a long-wheelbase edition of the CJ-5, and it had been intended from the beginning as a utility vehicle. The new model, however, was designed strictly as a pick-up truck on a long-wheelbase CJ chassis, and rather than a workhorse vehicle it was really a fashionable sportabout intended to appeal to a very different clientele. So, although it took on the CJ-8 designation, which was logical, Jeep generally referred to it by its marketing name of Scrambler.

The Scrambler had a wheelbase of 103.4in, which was a tenth of an inch less than the CJ-6 and exactly 10 inches

45

This CJ-8 sports a smart-looking hardtop.

more than the CJ-7. It had started life in the summer of 1979 as a plan to introduce a mini-truck to compete against Toyota's hugely successful 4x4 pick-ups, and the project had been given the go-ahead that September. In the beginning it was known as a CJ-6S, but as the project developed and used more CJ-7 components, it became clear that the vehicle was not a CJ-6 variant at all. So the CJ-8 designation was chosen before production began at Toledo in January 1981.

Like the CJ-7, the Scrambler used a boxed chassis-frame with semi-elliptic leaf springs all round, and had disc front brakes with drums at the rear. Its 5-foot pick-up bed was an integral part of the body structure, separated from the cab only by a low-height steel bulkhead. The basic body was open and doorless, but it was possible to buy a vinyl soft-top (with or without metal doors) and a removable GRP cab top which, like the hardtop option on the CJ-7, came with lockable steel doors.

Powertrain combinations were the same as on the CJ-7 of the time, with the four-cylinder Iron Duke as the base

engine and the 258ci six-cylinder as the option. From 1984, the Iron Duke was replaced by AMC's own four-cylinder. Four-speed manual transmissions were standard and three-speed automatics optional with both engines, although the six used heavier-duty items than the four in both cases. For 1982, the five-speed manual was also made optional. All the Scramblers came with a dual-range transfer gearbox and selectable four-wheel drive, and freewheeling front hubs were standard equipment.

The mini-truck market of the time demanded option packages in exactly the same way as the passenger car and 4x4 sport-utility markets, and so the Scrambler was offered with two unique packages, known as the SL Sport and SR Sport. The SR Sport was the less comprehensive, featuring special wheels and tyres, fender extensions, high-back bucket seats, a sports steering wheel and other trim items. The SL Sport package, meanwhile, brought chromed wheels, bumpers and grille, a soft or hard top with metal doors, and fender extensions over radial tyres. Inside, it featured high-back bucket seats, a leather-rimmed steering wheel, a centre console, a rev-counter and a clock. The graphics associated with these two packages changed for 1983, when the spare wheel on all models was relocated on the rollover bar. Then, for 1985, SL Sport and SR Sport gave way to Laredo and Renegade options.

On top of all these items, further options were available. On the mechanical side, there were of course alternative axle ratios, power-assisted brakes and power-assisted steering. On the borderline between the cosmetic and the practical came a tonneau cover, wooden side rails for the load bed and halogen foglamps. And, of course, buyers could order a stereo radio with either single-band (AM) or dual-band (AM and FM) reception. Yet the Scrambler was never available with some of the utility options which had been offered on the CJ-6 range, and most notably it was never offered with any power take-offs to suit the workhorse market at which the earlier vehicle had been aimed.

The Scrambler sold remarkably well over its five seasons of production, which broke into six calendar years. Sales were always considerably higher than those of the CJ-6s,

which demonstrated the truth of Jeep's belief that there was more money to be made from the fashion-conscious buyer than from the commercial utility market. It would be that belief, reflected in both the conception and the sales of the CJ-7 and Scrambler, which would shape the successors to the CJ range in the later 1980s and in the 1990s.

The YJ Wrangler, 1986-1996

Market research once again shaped the vehicle which replaced the CJ range in September 1986. According to François Castaing, the ex-Renault man then in charge of engineering and development at Jeep, 'the buyer profile of the small sport-utility has changed dramatically in recent years'. That statement was backed up with figures which showed that by the mid-1980s, 95% of Jeep owners were using their vehicles as everyday cars as opposed to just 17% in 1978. Whereas 37% of owners had regularly taken their vehicles off-road in 1978, only 7% did so by the mid-1980s, yet 80% of owners still wanted their Jeeps to have an off-road capability. The typical Jeep buyer of the mid-1980s

The old and the new: a late CJ-7 Renegade and a UK-registered YJ Wrangler.

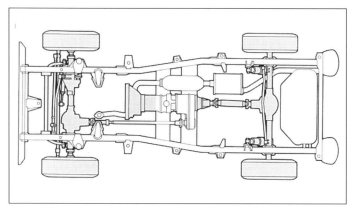

The YJ frame narrows towards the front, allowing for a tighter steering lock, while providing maximum strength and optimum spring location at the rear.

This 1989-model Wrangler S was the entry-level YJ of the time.

valued his vehicle's abilities, but was probably never going to use them – clearly a case of image triumphing over reality.

So when the successor to the CJ line was being designed in the first half of the 1980s, there was never any question that it might be offered as a commercial or utility model like the CJs of old. The new breed of Jeep buyer wanted an everyday car with all the excitement and image of the traditional Jeep, but without the drawbacks of its poor on-road ride, poor weatherproofing and general lack of refinement. So that was what Jeep came up with for the new YJ model, known more familiarly as the Wrangler.

From the beginning, it was clear that the YJ would use mechanical elements from the new XJ senior Jeep range, which was introduced for 1984 (*see Chapter 8*). In practice, however, the only engine borrowed from the XJ range for the first Wranglers was the 150ci four-cylinder. This became the base engine, and the option was the trusty AMC 258ci six. Transmission would be five-speed manual (an Aisin box on four-cylinders but a Peugeot one on sixes) and a three-speed automatic would be optional with the 258 engine. Command-Trac selectable four-wheel drive would be standard.

However, Jeep decided against using the pioneering unitary construction of the Cherokee in the Wrangler, reasoning that the open bodywork essential in any successor to the CJ line was likely to be too weak if the vehicle were to be used for heavy-duty off-road work. Instead, the Wrangler was built on a tough perimeter-frame chassis with rectangular-section side rails and four cross-members. Significantly, perhaps, it shared its 93.4in wheelbase with the CJ-7 it replaced. As on the XJ, there were live axles front and rear, but the Jeep engineers were unwilling to risk the coil-spring front suspension on a vehicle in the Wrangler's class, so the new model came with traditional semi-elliptic leaf springs on all four wheels. Nevertheless, a great deal of effort had been made to ensure that the on-road ride was better than that of the CJs. Panhard rods front and rear improved axle location, while an anti-roll bar on the front axle reduced the cornering roll so characteristic of the CJ line of Jeeps. Recirculating-ball steering, as pioneered on the CJ-7, gave quite accurate control and came with power assistance at extra cost – although it was then both rather too light and too quick on the road.

Further handling improvements resulted from the use of

Twin themes of travel and adventure inspired the packaging of the Wrangler Sahara soft-top pictured here.

low-profile tyres. While traditional 80-section tyres were of course the best for off-road use because they offered maximum ground clearance, low-profile tyres were expected on cars of the day. The Jeep designers therefore had to make a nod in that direction, and went as far as they dared by fitting the Wrangler with 75-section tyres. These came as standard with styled alloy wheels, with either a flat-spoke or a dished-spoke design. As for braking, there were still drums on the rear axle, but the front wheels carried ventilated discs, and power assistance was now standard.

There was no doubt that the Jeep engineers had made an excellent job of developing what was still in many ways a CJ Jeep into a vehicle whose road behaviour was in line with customer expectations of the mid-1980s. However, the chassis changes did have a downside in that they reduced both the suspension travel and the ground clearance. The result was that, while the Wrangler was as capable off-road as most buyers were likely to want, it did not have the same ability in extreme conditions as its CJ forebears.

As on the CJ line, the Wrangler's all-steel body tub was bolted to the chassis and came with a folding windscreen. Styling followed the broad outline of the CJ-7, but the traditional Jeep front panel now came with rectangular headlamps, and below them were rectangular direction indicator lamps. (For some export markets, however, there were direction indicator and driving lamp clusters sunk into the front of the wings instead.) The black fender extensions pioneered on special-edition CJ-7s had proved a big hit with the public, so the Wrangler had black plastic extensions as standard, blended into a sill strip under each door to give a continuity of line. These styling elements reduced the apparent height of the vehicle and gave a degree of protection against parking knocks.

The basic Wrangler body was an open tub, similar in concept to the traditional CJ type, and like the CJ-7 it could be fitted with either a soft-top or a removable hardtop. For safety reasons, both versions were equipped with a large rollover cage which was braced to the windscreen. For reasons of safety as well as refinement, both soft and hardtop versions came with steel doors – the first time proper doors had ever been offered on an open descendant

Special graphics on the hood, doors and spare wheel marked this YJ as the Islander model, which publicity described as 'an eye-catcher for the young buyer who appreciates four-wheel drive capability'.

This Renegade model from 1993 shows off the distinctive bodykit of the sporty YJ.

of the wartime MB. However, the doors differed between the two models. On the soft-top models, the doors reached only to the height of the rear body, and their leading edge was angled upwards to meet the base of the windscreen, so giving the impression of a rakish roadster-like cutaway door.

The doors which came with the hardtop – made of plastics composite like that on the CJ-7 – were taller, and their sheet metal was level with the base of the windscreen and the base of the side window in the hardtop. In addition, they included winding windows; soft-top buyers still had to make do with detachable sidescreens. Release handles were also different, though on both types they were flush-fitted 'letterbox' types, and the hinges of the hardtop model were covered with grey plastic shrouds while the soft-top's doors had exposed metal hinges.

Inside the body, the trim again made clear that the Jeep designers' aim had been to improve refinement. The standard high-back seats gave comfort undreamed of in most CJ models, and a completely redesigned instrument panel and control layout offered no surprises to the driver more used to a conventional car. Even with the optional soft-top (manufactured for Jeep by Bestop), weather-proofing was remarkably good, although of course noise levels were much lower with the hardtop option.

The Wrangler was introduced in May 1986, and from the beginning it was manufactured at the Brampton plant in Canada rather than at the traditional Jeep home of Toledo. It was initially available as a soft-top model to which a Sports Decor option package could be added, and as a more luxurious hardtop-only Laredo. The 1988 season introduced an additional Sahara model, finished in sand-coloured paint and hinting at the desert wildernesses of Africa. This was followed for 1989 by a stripped-out entry-level S model and by the Islander with bright yellow paint and colourful striping to suggest the carefree tropical islands. For the Renegade package, however, buyers had to wait a little longer – although their appetites were whetted by a concept car at the 1989 Detroit Auto Show, which was exhibited under the name of Rubicon.

Meanwhile, the 1990-season Wranglers benefited from door locks for soft-top models, more supportive high-back seats, a wash/wipe for the Laredo's hardtop and a bigger fuel tank for the Sahara and Laredo. But the big news was an engine change which brought even greater performance to the six-cylinder models, as the 258ci engine was replaced by the Cherokee's injected 4-litre (241ci) unit. Even though

Beginning with the 1993 model-year, the rear of the rollover cage was redesigned with a squarer section. Export models, like this 1994 RHD 4-litre Limited, also came with sidelamp and indicator clusters in the front fenders.

detuned from the Cherokee application, this still promised a massive 180bhp – which was more than the Wrangler needed and more than it could comfortably handle except in the hands of a sensible and experienced driver. At the same time, a new injection system boosted power of the four-cylinder engine to 123bhp.

The new six-cylinder engine was a big hit with Wrangler buyers and became standard in the Renegade package announced in January 1990 for the 1991 season. Renegades – the ultimate Wrangler for many buyers – were also distinguished by unique composite plastic mouldings running around the bottom of the body, which gave them a low-slung sporty appearance reminiscent more of a car than a red-blooded 4x4. Also part of the package were unique alloy wheels, a decorative stone shield under the body-coloured front bumper and additional driving lamps in the wing fronts.

All except the entry-level Wrangler S gained reclining bucket seats for 1991, a bigger centre console and the option of a 'sound bar' or speaker enclosure mounted on the rollover bar. Hardtops also became available for models other than the Laredo. A gauge package and new low-gloss

paints, plus a radio with clock function were 1992's novelties, but 1993 brought the more important option of ABS on six-cylinder Wranglers and a redesigned rollover cage for all models.

For 1994, automatic transmission became optional with the four-cylnder engine, and full-height metal doors became available with soft-tops. A high-mounted central brake light was added to the tailgate on a gooseneck bracket, and some model juggling saw the base Wrangler renamed an SE while a Sport option brought body colour fender flares and bodyside steps. Sales remained buoyant until production ended in 1996, when the model was replaced by the second-generation Wrangler, the TJ.

The Chrysler buy-out

The Jeep Corporation had prospered under AMC, and most particularly since Renault money had enabled the huge investment needed to get the XJ Cherokee range (*see Chapter 8*) into production in 1984. As already noted, the YJ Wrangler was developed using many of the XJ's mechanical components, and the mid-1980s saw Jeep sales climbing to new levels. This new-found success attracted

the interest of larger business combines, and in 1987 the Chrysler Corporation of Detroit put in a successful bid to purchase the Jeep marque (and, with it, the Eagle marque owned by AMC). The deal took effect from August 5 that year.

With the massive resources of Chrysler behind it, Jeep was in a better position than it had ever been. Since 1987, Chrysler's policy has been to expand Jeep sales by taking the marque into new areas. Thus, Chrysler funded the development of the 1992 ZJ Grand Cherokee (see Chapter 9) which enabled the Jeep marque to compete at the luxury end of the sport-utility wagon market. Beginning in 1988, Chrysler also made a determined attempt to become established in Europe, and its success was assisted in no small way by Jeep products.

This bid for sales in Europe had a number of by-products. One was that Jeep engines tended to be described in European terms; thus, Wranglers had 2.5-litre and 4-litre engines rather than 150ci and 241ci types. Another was that European requirements – including right-hand drive for Britain from 1992 – were incorporated at the design stage. This strategy inevitably made the products less

quintessentially American, but it did no more than reflect the decreasing insularity of the whole US motor industry and its acceptance of European and Japanese automotive design.

The Wrangler TJ

Jeep's engineers set themselves a hard task when they got down to creating the second-generation Wrangler. Their brief was to enhance every area of performance, safety and comfort, off-road capability and on-road refinement, and yet retain the essential character of the marque. And, as noted above, they had to ensure that the new model would appeal to European buyers as well as to Americans.

Nevertheless, Jeep's market researches showed that the customers were already happy with many aspects of the existing YJ Wrangler, and there was no point in making changes for change's sake. The powertrains already offered plenty of on-road performance and good lugging power for off-road work, so the existing 2.5-litre four-cylinder and 4-litre six-cylinder engines were retained for the new model. In line with current market trends, both were equipped with anti-theft immobilizers for the new vehicle. With them came

The TJ Wrangler reverted to the round headlamps beloved of Jeep traditionalists.

Coil springs for comfort, and now all this luxury! The interior of a RHD TJ reveals the modular dashboard and a standard of equipment quite unimaginable to the original buyers of CJ-2As some 50 years earlier.

the familiar five-speed manual transmission, three-speed automatic option and two-speed Command-Trac transfer box.

Buyers were also quite happy with the overall dimensions of the existing model, so for the third time the 93.4in wheelbase introduced with the CJ-7 some 20 years earlier was employed. Now under the overall direction of Chrysler's Trevor M Creed, the design engineers once again shied away from using unitary construction for an essentially open vehicle which was likely to take a severe pounding in off-road conditions. So the new TJ Wrangler was based on a rugged box-section chassis-frame with a separate steel body tub. However, the whole structure was strengthened to increase the rigidity necessary for more precise suspension tuning.

Perhaps most important, however, was that the traditional leaf springs of the CJ line were abandoned for coil springs all round. It is a moot point whether this change was actually forced upon Chrysler Jeep by competitive products (most notably from Land Rover, who had used coil-spring suspension since 1983). One way or another, though, the new suspension gave a much more car-like ride on the road and had the additional benefit of improving axle articulation for off-road work. All-coil suspension had already been seen on the 1992 Grand Cherokee (*see Chapter 9*), and for the TJ it was given the same descriptive name of Quadra-Coil.

The TJ Wrangler retained the successful styling of the YJ, with the main exception that round headlamps replaced the rectangular ones which many Jeep enthusiasts had felt detracted from the essential 'Jeepness' of the first-generation Wrangler. There was no doubt, too, that the American fashion for rectangular headlamps in the 1980s was not generally liked in Europe, and that the softer appearance of the round headlamps was likely to lead to greater acceptance of the TJ in this important market. Despite the styling similarities to the old model, however, almost all the exterior panels had been redesigned, only the doors and tailgate being carried over. Soft and hardtop options were available, as before, and both had been designed to be simpler to use. The soft-top was easier to raise and lower, while the hardtop was easier to remove and replace.

However, one area where the new Wrangler had undergone major change was in its interior. More space had been found within essentially the same dimensions as before, not least at the rear, where the new coil-spring suspension intruded less into the body space and permitted the rear seat to be wider. This seat, still a bench, now had a split-folding backrest to improve luggage space. Seat-belt pre-tensioners improved the safety equipment. A stereo radio was standard, and air conditioning – now integrated with the standard heating and ventilating system – was optional.

To meet forthcoming new safety regulations, it had been essential for the TJ to include driver and passenger airbags as standard, and in order to incorporate this technology the designers were obliged to redesign the dashboard completely. The design they chose was a modular one which made the parallel manufacture of left-hand drive and right-hand drive models simpler and cheaper than before, when completely different mouldings had been required. The new dashboard also transformed the appearance of the interior to make it much less spartan and truck-like. An adjustable steering column was of course part of the standard package.

The Wrangler TJ was announced at the Detroit Auto Show in January 1996, and became available later in the year as a 1997 model. It was made available for both left-hand drive and right-hand drive markets simultaneously – a first for a Jeep model.

CHAPTER 5

CJ derivatives

Dispatcher, Fleetvan, Forward Control and Jeepster Commando

The 1954 merger with Kaiser did the Jeep marque a power of good. The new Kaiser-Willys company took a long hard look at all the existing Jeep models and set about maximizing their sales potential in a way which Willys alone had never been able to do. The big Trucks, Station Wagons and Panel Deliveries (*see Chapter 6*) were given a much-needed shot in the arm when they were fitted with the Kaiser six-cylinder engine, and the strong-selling CJs were quickly exploited as the basis of further new models. Not all of these were very successful, but they all provided incremental sales at minimal cost to the company, and so helped to keep profits healthy.

The 1950s saw the introduction of two new CJ derivatives, while the 1960s witnessed the arrival of two more. First on the scene were the Dispatcher Jeeps, which arrived in 1955 and lasted through to 1973, when the company's new owners at American Motors dropped them from production. Next came the Forward Control Jeeps in 1956, which were not wholly successful and lasted only to 1964. Meanwhile, 1960 had seen the introduction of another short-lived model in the shape of the Fleetvan. Finally, 1967 brought the Jeepster Commando, which was axed at the same time as the Dispatcher models in 1973. Thereafter, as American Motors imposed their own strategies on the marque, there were no more of these fascinating oddities.

Dispatcher Jeeps

'The new 2-Wheel Drive "Jeep" Dispatcher offers

ruggedness and dependability characteristic of the built-in stamina for which the Willys "Jeep" Family of Vehicles are noted the world over . . . It fills the need for a two-wheel drive vehicle that will really take punishment.' So read an early sales brochure for the Jeep Dispatcher, making quite clear that the wartime qualities of dependability and ruggedness were still the best way to sell Jeeps, even in 1955!

Kaiser planned the Dispatcher as a low-cost delivery vehicle which was nimble enough to suit urban conditions and yet tough enough to take the hard knocks meted out to a commercial vehicle. In the words of that same brochure, it was 'the answer to transportation and delivery problems in highly congested metropolitan areas,' and 'America's lowest-priced delivery vehicle.' Manufacturing costs – and hence showroom costs – were minimized by using as many components as possible from the contemporary CJ models. There were deletions, too, because the Dispatcher needed only rear-wheel drive and so the four-wheel-drive transmission elements were omitted and the front axle was replaced by a solid I-beam drop-centre type. Road tyres of 6.40 size on 15in wheels also made quite clear that these models were not intended for the off-road conditions in which Jeep products traditionally excelled.

Nevertheless, the Dispatcher models also had a number of unique elements. From the beginning, they were available with four body styles, all based on the steel body tub of the CJ. The Hardtop was similar to the optional CJ-5 metal top and had the same sliding doors, but with a ribbed glassfibre roof. The remaining options were a Full Top, a Half Top, and a Convertible Top. The Full Top consisted of a canvas tilt which covered the front seats and extended to the rear of the vehicle, where its removable rear panel provided access to the load area. The Half Top provided a canvas roof, rear panel and sidescreens only for the driver and passenger compartment, and the Convertible Top folded neatly down with its tubular supporting frame to rest on top of the body sides at the rear of the vehicle. This configuration restricted cargo space a little, but was probably welcomed when vehicles were used for the dual role which Kaiser-Willys advertising envisaged, for the copywriters had spotted the recreational value of this little open vehicle: 'The sporty, continental lines of the Soft-top Dispatcher appeal to the fun-loving Prep School and College Set.'

The first Dispatchers were announced in 1955 and were known as DJ-3A models. By this time, the regular production CJ was the CJ-3B, with its Hurricane engine and taller bonnet, but the Dispatcher used the older (and

Among the strangest versions of the CJ models were the two-wheel-drive Dispatchers. This is the 1960-model DJ-3A Surrey, complete with fringed canvas top.

Preserved DJ-5 Dispatcher in original US Mail livery. The large mirrors on the windscreen pillar and LH wing were to help the driver to pull out safely despite the handicap of RH drive.

cheaper) Go-Devil four-cylinder engine under the lower bonnet of the superseded CJ-3A. Its model designation therefore made perfect sense. DJ-3A models remained available until 1965 and were by far the most numerous of the Dispatcher types. They included a few hundred examples of an intriguing runabout introduced in 1959 and equipped with a striped Surrey top and striped upholstery. Initially known as the Jeep Gala and available only in pink (with white stripes), it was renamed the Surrey for the 1960 season when blue and green were added to the colour options. Most found use on golf courses and at holiday resorts, and one hotel in the Mexican resort of Acapulco operated a whole fleet of them.

In 1964, just before the final DJ-3As were made, Kaiser-Willys announced their replacement in the shape of the DJ-5A. Not surprisingly, this had the same relationship to the contemporary CJ-5 as the DJ-3A had to the CJ-3A. A year later came a second model, the DJ-6A, which was based on the 101in wheelbase CJ-6. Among the DJ-5A variants was the Dispatcher 100, which was bought in quantity by the US Postal Service. This came with the hardtop and sliding doors and had right-hand drive: the theory was that the postman could drive along his route and simply lean out of the window to deliver the mail to kerbside mailboxes!

A total of 22,264 Dispatchers were sold in 18 years, but sales had slowed up long before production was halted. Average annual sales of the DJ-3A had been around 1,360 in the 10 years of its availability, but over the next nine years the annual sales average of DJ-5A and DJ-6A combined was well below 1,000. American Motors, more interested in tackling the growing sport-utility market than in exploiting niche markets as Kaiser had done, decided not to carry on with the Dispatchers and the last examples were made in 1973.

The Forward Controls
With the Dispatchers well on their way to success, the new Kaiser team at Willys turned their attention to a different area of the commercial vehicle market. One of the problems with many commercial vehicles was their size, and in order to reduce overall length the manufacturers of larger vehicles

This 1975 DJ-5A started life with the US Postal Service, and always had right-hand drive. Now preserved by an enthusiast in the UK, it wears aftermarket wheels it never had when new.

had long ago begun to exploit the forward-control layout, in which the driver sat alongside or over the engine rather than behind it as in a conventional car. There seemed to be potential for a much smaller vehicle which would make the most efficient use of the space available within its 'footprint' by using a forward-control layout, and so the designers set about developing forward-control versions of the CJ Jeeps.

From the beginning, the vehicles were intended to use as many standard CJ components as possible, in order to minimize manufacturing costs. Two different basic models were developed. The smaller FC-150 used the 81in wheelbase CJ-5 chassis with the four-cylinder Hurricane engine, and had a 74in truck bed with a ¾-ton payload. The

There was no mistaking the FC Jeeps for anything else. This is the short-wheelbase FC-150 variant, based on a CJ-5 chassis. The cab was common to both FC-150 and FC-170 models.

larger FC-170, meanwhile, had a 9ft cargo box and was based on the 101in wheelbase CJ-6 chassis – although its wheelbase actually ended up as 103.5in, probably to make room for the ex-Kaiser six-cylinder Super Hurricane engine. A single-lever transfer box was used, incorporating an innovative shift-on-the-fly system, which allowed four-wheel drive to be engaged or disengaged without stopping the vehicle.

The rest of the redesign was minimal: the driving compartment was moved forwards and above the engine, while a series of special linkages restored steering, gear and braking controls. Then a special cab, which looked like nothing else associated with the Jeep marque before or since, was created to encase the engine and driving compartment. A De Luxe option included extra rear side windows, which made a big difference to the driver's ability to see out of the back. A variety of rear body styles could be specified, and the Forward Control Jeeps were also sold in chassis-cab form for special bodywork to be fitted.

The FC-150 was introduced at the end of November 1956 and was only ever available with four-wheel drive. The FC-170, which followed a month later, could be bought with either a 4x2 or a 4x4 transmission. For certain tasks, these vehicles were ideal, and the FC-170 in particular made a useful compact fire truck, in which guise it was most commonly fitted with the dual rear wheel option introduced in 1960. The US military also took a number of FC-170s, fitted with diesel engines and mostly bodied as crew-cab pick-ups or ambulances.

However, the Forward Control Jeeps did have a number of drawbacks. Stability on side slopes was one as the vehicles were much taller than the CJs on which they were based. Without a heavy rear body, most of their weight was also over the front axle, which led to braking and handling problems, though Kaiser-Willys attempted to alleviate this by fitting counterweights at the rear of the chassis on some vehicles. This weight imbalance also led to failures in the front suspension and steering. Finally, the Forward Control Jeeps had low gearing to cope with the heavy payloads which their designers anticipated, but this meant that their top speed was limited to an unacceptable degree for anything other than local journeys.

After 1957 had seen an encouraging initial flurry of interest, with 6,637 FC-150s and 3,101 FC-170s finding buyers, the news of these shortcomings spread. The figures for 1958 showed an alarming drop, to 2,072 FC-150s and 1,522 FC-170s, and sales never did recover. Nevertheless, the Forward Control Jeeps remained available until 1964, when Kaiser-Willys decided to cut its losses and discontinued both models. Full production figures are not available, but it is unlikely that the overall total was greater than about 30,000.

In keeping with its policy of licensing overseas manufacture of Jeep products, Kaiser-Willys licensed the Mahindra company to build a version of the Forward Control Jeep in India. The Indian vehicle was known as an FC-160 and had a different specification from the Toledo-built types, with a 92in wheelbase and four-cylinder Hurricane engine. No production figures for this variant are available.

The Fleetvan

In July 1960, the US Postal Service placed the first of a series of orders for a model known as the FJ-3A Fleetvan. Developed specially to meet postal requirements, this was based on the 81in wheelbase CJ-5 chassis, converted to forward-control layout and rear-wheel drive and fitted with the Huricane four-cylinder engine. The chassis was clothed in a tall walk-through van body with sliding cab access doors and an angular windscreen glass arrangement. Once again, the vehicle was totally unlike anything else produced under the Jeep name, and would have been unrecognizable as a Jeep product without the small badge above its radiator air intake which read 'Jeep Fleetvan'.

Kaiser-Willys had high hopes that the FJ-3A would find a niche in the urban delivery van market, and made it available to non-Government customers for the 1961 model-year. Despite a 170cu ft cargo area, however, the van was perceived as too small and its payload as too low. So the Fleetvan remained a rarity, and today is one of the forgotten Jeeps.

Two views of an FC-170 Stake Truck, which has been preserved by a UK enthusiast. It has the standard single-rear-wheel specification.

The FC-170 with dual rear wheels was often seen as a fire truck. This example dates from 1964, the last year of production.

The Jeepster Convertible, Jeepster Commando and the Commando

With the sport-utility market opening up in a big way in the mid-1960s, as International scored a hit with the Scout and Ford followed up with the Bronco, Kaiser-Willys determined to claim their share of sales. While the Wagoneer was in many ways one of the vehicles which had made the market possible in the first place, it was a much bigger vehicle than the Ford, which appealed through its combination of versatility and handiness. So the Toledo design engineers set to work on a Jeep sport-utility which would give the marque a presence in the new market. They announced it in February 1967 in two versions, both using the once-famous name of Jeepster.

In order to save both development time and costs, the Jeep engineers had adapted existing hardware wherever they could. Thus, the Jeepster's chassis-frame was essentially the CJ-6 type with boxed-in side-members and 101in wheelbase, but the rear springs were mounted on outriggers to improve the handling. The base engine was the faithful Hurricane four-cylinder, but the optional 160bhp Dauntless V6 inevitably proved more popular and was the only one which lived up to Jeep's advertising of the vehicle as a 'bold new sports car'. All models had four-wheel drive with a two-speed transfer case operated by the single-lever control pioneered on the Wagoneer. A three-speed primary gearbox was standard with both engines, with the gearshift normally on the column, but optionally in a neat floor-mounted console to suit the fashion of the times. The V6 could be ordered optionally with the Turbo-Hydramatic three-speed automatic, again with a console-mounted shifter.

The Jeepster's front panels left no doubt about its family identity, although they were actually unique to the model. They were modified versions of the CJ-5 and CJ-6 style, differing through a wider hood and a matching wider section at the top of the grille panel, which allowed for the indicator lamps to be sited high up alongside the headlamps rather than below them as on the CJs. Behind the single-pane windscreen, the flat-panelled open two-door bodywork hinted at the Brooks Stevens-designed Jeepster of the late 1940s. It featured steel doors with winding windows, and an interior which was much more plush than the regular CJs boasted at the time. All upholstery was in vinyl, with matching door trim panels and quarter-trim pads. Bucket front seats were optional, and the standard bench had a one-third/two-thirds split, the single third on the passenger side folding forwards to allow access to the rear bench seat.

The Jeepster came in two main versions, called the Jeepster Convertible and the Jeepster Commando. Both were known to Kaiser-Willys as C-101 models. The more expensive Convertible had a folding top which could be ordered with the option of power operation, and this folded down into a lidded well behind the rear seats. To give a neater appearance and to blend in with the soft-top, the upper panelwork of Convertible bodies was painted white around the passenger area. In addition, the Convertible carried its spare wheel externally on the tail panel,

Continental-style. Options included de luxe interior trim, spoked wheel covers (designed to resemble the fashionable sporty magnesium alloy wheels of the time) and air conditioning.

The white paint was absent from the upper panels of the Commando version, which carried its spare wheel inside the body behind the rear seats and came with three different body configurations. As a basic open two-door body, it was a roadster. Fitting a soft or hard cab top and removing the rear seat turned it into a pick-up, and finally adding a full-length GRP hardtop turned it into a station wagon. This versatility, of course, was not unique to Jeep: the International Scout, against which the Jeepster models were ranged, had pioneered a similar range of body styles some years earlier. Commando models could also be fitted with a De Luxe trim package which was not available on the Convertibles.

The new Jeepsters were welcomed enthusiastically in the motoring media, but sales did not match Kaiser-Willys' expectations. So in June 1968 (when it qualified as a '1968½' model), the Jeepster Convertible was revised. Its convertible top was given a more sporty, raked rear panel; the spare wheel was relocated more conventionally and the rear panel was given a hinged tailgate.

Over the next couple of years, Jeep did what they could to sell the Jeepsters. Power-assisted steering was made optional for 1969 with the V6 engine. Convertibles lost their white upper panels, and the development of a limited-edition sporty model was initiated under Kaiser and taken up enthusiastically by AMC. When it was announced in July 1970 as a 1971 model, this carried the name of Hurst Jeepster Special. Hurst, of course, were specialists in floor-shift conversions among other things, and they had previously worked with AMC on some sporty versions of the company's cars. There were plans to build 500 examples of the Hurst Jeepster Special, although some sources suggest that no more than 100 were ever made.

The Hurst Jeepster Special was finished in Champagne White with blue and red rally stripes across the cowl and tailgate, and featured a vacuum-formed ABS plastic hood scoop which incorporated an 8,000rpm rev-counter ahead

The Jeepster Commando Station Wagon was an early attempt at a sport-utility model. The roof section was always finished in white, as on this 1969 example.

of the driver in the latest fashion. Six-inch wheel rims with special Goodyear tyres, and a padded steering wheel with brushed chrome spokes, were also part of the equipment. All examples had the Dauntless V6 engine, and the plan was for 300 to have automatic transmission with a Hurst Dual Gate shifter (which allowed full manual control of the gearbox), and for the other 200 to have the manual transmission with Hurst's famous T-handle gear lever.

The Hurst special-edition failed to revitalize sales, which actually started to slide during 1971. Fortunately, AMC were already working on revised Jeepsters for introduction in July 1972 as 1973 models. These would have AMC's own engines, would incorporate a number of other modifications to suit, and would come with a new name and different model availability.

The new name was quite simply Jeep Commando; the Jeepster name had been dropped. The Convertible model

Interior styling of the Jeepster Commando was car-like, with full door trim and comfortable seats. The dashboard, however, was resolutely spartan.

While the Jeepster Commando was undeniably able off-road, its bland styling cannot have helped sales. Front-end styling of the Jeepster Commando recalled the classic CJs, but had its own distinctive details.

had also been abandoned, and the Commandos were available only as roadster, pick-up or station wagon. They had a thoroughly revised front end, modified mainly to allow the longer AMC six-cylinder engines to be installed under the hood. The wheelbase had been stretched by 3 inches to make 104in, and the revised models were known by their manufacturers as C-104 types. With the stretched wheelbase came the latest Dana 30 open-knuckle front axle, which increased the track slightly but permitted a much tighter steering lock; the Dana 44 axle at the rear remained unchanged. Most obviously, however, the CJ-type front-end styling had been banished, and the Commandos had full-width nose styling which brought them into line with the small pick-up trucks of the day. The new nose carried a pressed steel grille with a rectangular

cross-hatch pattern.

The Commandos could be bought with a new heavy-duty rear spring option to increase their payload. They could also be ordered with a Decor Group, which included a cigarette lighter, wheel covers, chrome bumpers, armrests and vinyl overmats. While the transmission choices were unchanged, there were now three engine options: AMC's 100bhp 232ci six, its 110bhp 258ci six, and at the top its 150bhp 304ci V8.

The powerful AMC engines certainly made the Commando a more attractive vehicle than it had been, but despite improved sales at the tail end of 1972 and during 1973, it was dropped from production in the summer of that year. AMC had probably seen it purely as a stop-gap model while a more credible contender was developed for the sport-utility market, and that – the Cherokee which was introduced immediately after the Commandos disappeared from the showrooms – proved a much more successful vehicle.

CHAPTER 6

The senior Jeeps (1)

Wagon, Panel Delivery, Truck and Jeepster

The industrial designer Brooks Stevens had a major impact on the postwar destiny of the Jeep. In 1942 he presented a paper to the Society of Automotive Engineers about the potential civilian uses of the wartime runabout, and in the December 1942 issue of *Popular Mechanics* magazine he further expounded these ideas in an article. His ideas came to the attention of Barney Roos, the Engineering Vice President of Willys Overland, and Roos hired him to assist with the development of ideas for the peacetime Jeep and to look at the design of future new Willys sedan models.

At about the same time, John Tjaarda (of Lincoln Zephyr fame) proposed to Willys' Chairman, Ward Canaday, that the company should market a civilianized Jeep, a long-wheelbase Jeep derivative with a plywood station wagon body, and a two-wheel-drive passenger car derivative of the Jeep. The civilianized MB was already a certainty by this time, and no formal agreement seems to have been reached between Willys and Tjaarda, but there seems little doubt that his proposals left their mark. Within five years, Willys had developed and introduced both a long-wheelbase Jeep Station Wagon and a two-wheel-drive passenger car variant known as the Jeepster.

Nothing very tangible seems to have happened until 1944, when Willys' President, Joseph W Frazer, left to go into partnership with industrial magnate Henry J Kaiser and Charles 'Cast Iron Charlie' Sorensen took over. Sorensen instructed Brooks Stevens to abandon all work on the sedan models which were already running in prototype form. His view was that Willys Overland was not big enough to compete with Detroit's Big Three manufacturers at their own game. However, the Jeep had earned – and was still earning – a formidable reputation, which Willys would be foolish not to exploit. So, he insisted, Willys should concentrate the whole of their efforts on Jeep-derived products for the immediate postwar period.

The Station Wagon, 1946-1955

Sorensen wanted to build not only the civilianized MB Jeep, which eventually became the CJ-2A, but he also wanted to make a long-wheelbase station wagon derivative as well as a pick-up based on this. As the Jeep's reputation would be vital in the success of the new models, he insisted that they should have front panels which made clear their relationship to the wartime legend. All American station wagon bodies of the period had wooden construction, but Sorensen believed that such a body would not have the durability associated with the Jeep, and so he wanted the Jeep Station Wagon's body to be made of steel.

A problem now arose. Willys Overland had been sinking fast when the war broke out, and even the success of the military Jeep had not eradicated industry suspicions that the company was on the brink of failure. Willys did not have their own body plant (and would not do so until 1949), and so were dependent on bought-in body pressings. Yet none of the major specialist companies wanted to risk working with a small manufacturer whose future survival was questionable. So Willys were forced to deal with smaller body pressing companies, which were unable to produce

Discover how useful a car can be

'Jeep' Station Wagon

NO WONDER 'Jeep' Station Wagon owners marvel at their gas mileage! At speeds above 30, an overdrive cuts engine speed 30%, traveling you 42% farther for every turn of the engine.

WITH SEATS REMOVED, you have 98 cubic feet of load space, more with the tailgate lowered. Seats and interior are washable. It's a truly useful car, with double utility for greater value.

Talk to 'Jeep' Station Wagon owners to discover how useful a car can be—how economical and all-around satisfying.

They'll tell you it's grand for families—a comfortable passenger car, with upholstery children won't harm . . . and, with seats out, a practical vehicle for hauling, too.

Women will tell you how easily it handles, how smoothly it rides on rough roads. Men will brag on mileage and low maintenance.

See it now at Willys-Overland dealers—the *first* station wagon with an all-steel body.

THE NEW *Jeep' Station Sedan* is an entirely new type of car . . . giving you the spaciousness of a station wagon and the luxurious comfort of a sedan. There is unusual leg and head room for six in its all-steel body, plus a large, accessible luggage space. Its new Willys-Overland '6' Engine, with overdrive, gives smooth performance, together with remarkable gasoline mileage. You'll like everything about it, including its smart styling.

WILLYS-OVERLAND MOTORS, TOLEDO · MAKERS OF AMERICA'S MOST USEFUL VEHICLES

This advertisement for the Station Wagon and the then-new Station Sedan ran in a number of publications in October-November 1948.

pressings as complicated as those which the big firms could manufacture.

Brooks Stevens was therefore instructed to design an all-steel station wagon body which could be made up of panels with no more than a 6in 'draw' – the best that the small

pressing companies could offer. He was told that the chassis would have a 104in wheelbase, and was left to get on with the job. So the body he first sketched in 1944 had extremely simple styling to match the simple pressings which would be available. From the beginning, he also designed it to look as if it had traditional wooden construction, although the 'framework' visible was actually no more than extrusions on the steel panels which served both to reinforce them and to add visual interest. On the earliest Station Wagons, the body sides were actually painted to look like mahogany, while lighter paint on the extruded pressings suggested a beech or ash frame! The main panels, meanwhile, were finished in a deep burgundy called Luzon Red. In fact, the 1946 Jeep Station Wagon represented an industry 'first'. Not until 1949 would another manufacturer in the USA offer an all-steel station wagon, and the Plymouth Suburban which arrived that year was really a very different kind of vehicle, much more like a conventional sedan.

The body of the Jeep Station Wagon was tall and angular, and had just two doors – there never would be a four-door model – and a horizontally split tailgate. It was designed to seat five or six passengers in reasonable comfort, while offering a very large load area behind the rear seats. A folding 'occasional' seventh seat could be fitted in the load bed of 1946 and early 1947 models. There were two individual front seats, set close together so that a third passenger could sit in the middle if necessary (though he had to be friendly with the floor-mounted gear lever), and the rear seat was a bench type wide enough to accommodate three people. However, it was a bench with a difference: the seat was split into two sections, which could be folded forward or removed altogether independently of one another. The dividing line set one-third of the bench on the left of the vehicle and two-thirds on the right, thus making for maximum flexibility of the big load area behind the front seats.

As the new big Jeep was primarily a passenger-carrying vehicle, it was kitted out to look less spartan than the CJs and military models, and items such as chromed hubcaps and bumpers were standard wear from the beginning. Early

The Station Wagon was designed for both suburban and rural use, but this 1946 two-wheel-drive version might have had some difficulty in the snow chosen as the setting for this publicity picture.

models had a plain design of front bumper, but by 1948 a large overrider bar had become standard. Nevertheless, the essentially spartan nature of its ancestor was reflected in such things as the resolutely simple instrumentation, which went through minor variations over the years but was always placed centrally on the dashboard and was always dominated by a large speedometer.

The new chassis-frame developed for the Station Wagon was also used for the Panel Delivery model, which was based on the Station Wagon's body, and versions of it would see use in the pick-up truck and sporty Jeepster derivatives. Though hardly updated at all, it survived for 19 years in its various guises – a production run which attests to the soundness of its basic design. In essence, it was of course a Jeep chassis stretched by 2ft to give the same 104in wheelbase as the 1941 Willys American. However, the stretch involved more than just a simple lengthening of the side rails, which were boxed to give additional strength, while a large X-shaped brace was added in the centre.

Even though four-wheel drive was an integral part of what had made the Jeep great, Willys Overland decided to introduce the Station Wagons with two-wheel drive only. In an attempt to improve ride quality, they also fitted them with a crude independent front suspension system called Planadyne, which consisted of a single transverse seven-leaf spring with control arms to locate each wheel. This had been designed by Barney Roos, and was similar to the Planar design he had drawn up for Studebaker in the 1930s. The Jeep Trucks, meanwhile, introduced in 1947, were equipped with the familiar Jeep four-wheel drive system and leaf-sprung live axles both front and rear, and in July 1949 this became available on Station Wagons. The 4x4 Wagons sold relatively poorly at first, but sales soon picked up and in 1952 the 4x4 models outsold the 4x2 types for the first time. Over the years, it was the four-wheel-drive models which proved by far the more popular. Two-wheel-drive models nevertheless remained available all the way through to 1965, though after 1955 a conventional beam front axle replaced the trouble-prone Planadyne independent front end.

In the beginning, all the Station Wagons were powered by the four-cylinder Go-Devil engine, which was reliable enough, but with 63bhp was no great performer in a vehicle 600lb heavier than a CJ-2A, even before it was laden with passengers and luggage. Rather better was the 72bhp six-cylinder alternative introduced in 1948 and known as the Lightning, although the taller gearing which came with this and was intended to give a more relaxed cruising speed nullified some of the new engine's advantages. Designed by Barney Roos, the 148.5ci (2.4-litre) Lightning engine was the smallest six-cylinder then in production in the USA. Otherwise, however, it was a curious mix of the conventional and the modern, mixing side-valves with the latest thinwall casting technology and siamesed bores. Mostly, what it brought to the senior Jeep models was a degree of refinement which was lacking in the Go-Devil four-cylinder.

Refinement was the name of the game for Willys at this stage, however, and the company decided to try its luck for 1948 with a de luxe version of the Station Wagon, known as the Station Sedan. This had a chromed facing on the grille, a more luxurious interior with cloth upholstery, and a special paint job which had imitation basket-weave panels between the pressed 'framework' mouldings of the side panels. The model was withdrawn after just two seasons, however. All Station Sedans had the six-cylinder engine, and so their grille did not carry the identifying badge used on other long-wheelbase models built between 1948 and 1950. These were an encircled 4 or 6, fitted at the top of the grille panel to indicate whether the four-cylinder Go-Devil or six-cylinder Lightning engine was fitted.

The 1950 season proved to be an important watershed for all the long-wheelbase Jeep models. Visually, it brought a new vee-shaped grille with five horizontal chromed bars, which together with more pointed fender fronts gave the nose a more aggressive and less utilitarian appearance. Squared-off rear wheelarches also replaced the original round ones. Mechanically, it brought the more powerful Hurricane four-cylinder engine in place of the venerable Go-Devil. This was a welcome improvement, but it did not solve the fundamental problem that these big Jeeps were drastically underpowered. The Hurricane, seen also in the M-38A1 military Jeep and the CJ-3B during this period, brought 73bhp in place of the Go-Devil's 63bhp, but its arrival was a case of too little, too late.

The six-cylinder Lightning engine was revised at the same time, taking on the new F-head configuration developed for the Hurricane and being bored out to take the Hurricane's pistons. In big-bore guise, it had a swept volume of 161ci (2.6 litres), but it offered no more power than the smaller-capacity original. An opportunity had been missed because of Willys Overland's desire to save money through component standardization, and the disappointing performance of the six-cylinder Station Wagons would dog their sales for years. The four-cylinder versions would always out-sell them until a completely new six-cylinder engine was introduced in 1954.

In terms of sales, 1950 was a watershed year which saw sales peak at 39,911 vehicles (including Panel Delivery models). In 1951, sales of the closed-body long-wheelbase Jeeps slipped by a little under 10%, then crashed to just 33% of the 1951 total in 1952. The following year brought a small revival, mainly through 4x4 models with the Hurricane engine, which had just been uprated to 75bhp, and this gave Willys a clear indication that the market wanted more power harnessed to four-wheel drive. Hurricane-engined 4x4 Station Wagons were again the best sellers in 1954, but the overall sales total for that year (again including Panel Delivery models) was an abysmal 7,116. This was barely more than the 6,534 sold in 1946, when the big Jeeps had been introduced part-way through the calendar year.

This sales slide was abruptly arrested after the 1954 Kaiser takeover. One of the first things which Kaiser did was to equip the long-wheelbase models with a new and more powerful six-cylinder engine from its own product range, and the new management also introduced marketing strategies which made the most of the undoubted strengths of the big Jeep. For the first time, the Station Wagon/Sedan Delivery chassis was offered in bodyless form to enable specialist converters to create bespoke vehicles for their clients. In addition, the all-steel closed body was exploited as the basis of ambulance conversions, and although neither these nor the bare chassis brought in more than a handful of sales each year, they did help to emphasise the versatility of the big Jeep and probably gathered extra sales of the standard variants in the process.

The Kaiser six-cylinder engine which replaced the 161ci Willys engine in the 104in wheelbase Jeeps during 1954 had a swept volume of 226ci (3.7 litres) and pumped out a very healthy 115bhp. Even more important, its torque of 190lb.ft at a low 1,800rpm was in a different league from anything Willys had fielded in a Jeep product before. The result was to give the Station Wagons the sort of performance they had cried out for from the beginning. Kaiser management was also astute enough to recognize that adding the four-wheel drive option not available with the earlier six-cylinder engines would meet the market demand for power coupled to a 4x4 transmission, which 1953's sales results had demonstrated so graphically. Their guess was right on target, and from 1955 the four-wheel-drive six-cylinder variant became the best-selling Jeep Station Wagon, a status it retained until the end of production.

When fitted to the long-wheelbase Jeep chassis, the Kaiser six-cylinder engine was known as the Super Hurricane, which was a rather misleading name as it had absolutely nothing in common with the four-cylinder Hurricane engine. Nor did its origins have much to do with Kaiser, as it happens. The engine had been designed by Continental many years earlier, and been manufactured and sold by that company as the Red Seal industrial engine before being bought by the Kaiser-Frazer Corporation at the end of the Second World War. Kaiser-Frazer had redeveloped it for automotive use and fitted it to both Kaiser and Frazer saloons from 1946 through to 1955, when saloon car production stopped. So it was a well-tried engine by the time Willys were able to make use of it, and it remained the staple power unit of the Station Wagon and Sedan Delivery ranges until 1962, when it was replaced by the even more powerful Tornado overhead-camshaft six-cylinder engine.

The Super Hurricane six-cylinder engine which came as part of the deal with Kaiser made an enormous difference to the performance of these big Jeeps.

The Utility Wagon, 1956-1965

Meanwhile, Kaiser marketing policies continued to have a beneficial effect on sales of the Jeep Station Wagon. The model was simplified for 1956 and renamed the Utility Wagon. It retained four-wheel drive, but lost cosmetic items like the chromed hubcaps of the earlier Station Wagons, and carried the simpler front and rear bumpers associated with the Sedan Delivery. The grille was simplified, with three chromed bars instead of five; the inward-facing seventh seat in the load area was deleted; and overdrive became optional instead of standard. Utility Wagons were also listed with workhorse options such as a PTO and snow-plough, which remained available until production ended nine years later.

The Utility Wagons changed little for the rest of the

Designer Brooks Stevens poses with the limited-edition Harlequin, a transitional model with the single-pane windscreen but two-pane tailgate.

decade, but at the end of the 1950s Kaiser experimented with a pair of special editions. The first, called the Harlequin, was introduced late in the 1959 season, apparently to test the market for more luxurious station wagons once again. Featuring special exterior trim and upholstery with a Harlequin diamond pattern, both the work of designer Brooks Stevens, it also carried chromed hubcaps with special harlequin centre caps. The second re-introduced two-wheel drive to the Utility Wagon and was an entry-level model with the four-cylinder engine called the Maverick Special; it was introduced mid-way through the 1960 season. The name came from Kaiser-Willys' sponsorship of the *Maverick* TV programme. Among other things, the Maverick had special side mouldings delineating a pencil shape at waist height to permit the use of fashionable two-tone colour schemes. Things had certainly come a long way since the MB had been available in just one colour – military khaki!

It was in 1960, too, that a single-pane windscreen replaced the two-pane type standard since the beginning in 1946, and this had a surprisingly modernizing effect on the now ageing Utility Wagon design. Slightly later, the two-pane glass in the upper tailgate also gave way to a single pane. As part of the 1960 facelift, Kaiser-Willys added an angled moulding which followed the line of the front wing's trailing edge and then swept back at the height of the wing top to form the colour boundary for a different style of two-tone colour split. The wooden slats were also deleted from the rear load floor, and the rear seating arrangement was changed to give the one-third seat on the right-hand side and the two-thirds on the left. Better carpets were introduced, and a 'breathing' upholstery fabric was standardized.

The final revisions came in 1962, when the Super Hurricane six-cylinder engine was replaced by a new and even more powerful overhead-camshaft six-cylinder known as the Tornado. This 140bhp motor had really been designed for the new generation of big Jeeps that would make their bow during 1963 for the 1964 season, and is described in more detail in Chapter 7. During 1963, the Utility Wagons were also given a new pencil-shaped side moulding similar to that first seen on the 1960 Maverick

Early 1960s two-toning helps this rather run-down Utility Wagon retain a certain rugged elegance.

model. The last one did not roll off the assembly lines until 1965, but by then sales had dwindled almost to nothing in the wake of the Wagoneer's arrival for 1963.

Willys Rural
From 1958, a version of the six-cylinder Station Wagon with four-wheel drive was built by Willys do Brasil for the domestic market. This was known as the Willys Rural, and resembled the Toledo-built original in general outline but featured a distinctive front-end design, once again by Brooks Stevens. It was available with both four-wheel-drive and rear-wheel-drive transmissions. After the Ford and Willys interests in Brazil were merged in 1968, the Rural – still in production even though Station Wagons had long since stopped coming off the assembly lines in Toledo – was rebadged as a Ford-Willys.

The Panel Delivery
The Panel Delivery introduced in 1947 was essentially a Jeep Station Wagon with plain metal panels in place of the rear side windows, vertically split rear doors, no rear seat

and simpler bumpers. Designed to be built on the same tooling in order to minimize production costs, it was a capacious commercial vehicle. Precise sales figures in the early days cannot be determined because they are not separated from those of the Station Wagons, but the Panel Delivery probably found no more than a few hundred buyers every year until it was given a new lease of life under Kaiser ownership of Willys in the mid-1950s.

New models introduced in the early 1950s suggest that sales of the Panel Delivery were then sliding in the same way as those of the Station Wagon. The model was grandly renamed a Sedan Delivery for 1952 and became available with a number of cosmetic options in an attempt to boost sales. For 1953, a four-wheel-drive version was added to the catalogue, and for 1954 the six-cylinder engine became optional on rear-wheel-drive models. None of these ploys seems to have been very effective, however.

Kaiser's new policies and the six-cylinder engine which it bequeathed to the Sedan Delivery under the Super Hurricane name quickly had an impact on sales. During 1955, the combination of Super Hurricane engine and 4x4

Rugged and businesslike, this is the four-wheel-drive Jeep Truck. Note the cab door, shared with the Station Wagons, and the '4-Wheel-Drive' badge on the hood. This 1950 example was brought across to the UK by an enthusiast.

The three chromed bars on the grille of this Jeep Truck make clear that it dates from 1956 or later.

transmission accounted for a massive 5,890 Sedan Delivery sales, but this total was never again approached and subsequent annual sales rarely exceeded 1,000 units. A few six-cylinder Sedan Delivery models were supplied as ambulances – a role for which they were admirably equipped – and Kaiser's insistence on offering bare chassis and chassis-cowls for bodying by specialists found a handful of extra sales each year. The Sedan Delivery models were phased out in 1962, but not before the arrival of the new Tornado six-cylinder engine, which was offered with both rear-wheel and four-wheel drive on the final examples made over the summer of that year.

The Jeep Truck

From 1947, the chassis of the big Jeeps was stretched to a wheelbase of 118in for a second commercial vehicle, this time a rugged pick-up truck. The styling of the front panels and cab was shared with the Station Wagon and Panel Delivery models, and Trucks even had the Station Wagon doors complete with their fake wooden frame pressings. From 1950, however, the grille styling differed, as Trucks had painted horizontal bars on the vee-grille rather than the chromed type on Station Wagons.

All the factory-bodied Jeep Trucks were equipped with an enclosed cab with two or three seats. The rear of the chassis could nevertheless be fitted with a variety of different bodies.

Most popular over the years were the pick-ups and stake trucks, but chassis-cowl and bare chassis versions also became available in the early 1950s, and a number of Jeep Trucks were equipped with specialist bodywork. Several were also turned into ambulances and, after Kaiser began marketing the model more aggressively in 1955, into fire trucks.

In the beginning, the Trucks were available with both two-wheel and four-wheel drive, the former with a 1-ton payload and the latter with a ¾-ton rating. The two-wheel-drive models just outsold the 4x4s in 1946, but after that the four-wheel-drive models proved by far the more popular. Indeed, after 1952, four-wheel drive was part of the Truck's standard specification, and the two-wheel-drive models were built only to special order. The 4x4 models always had the Borg-Warner T-90 gearbox, a Spicer Model 18 transfer box and, of course, Spicer axles front and rear.

Jeep Truck engine development followed much the same route as the Station Wagons, but neither version of the Lightning six-cylinder engine was ever available in these models. The Go-Devil four-cylinder was the sole option until the Hurricane four-cylinder took over for the 1951 season. That engine remained available right through to the end of production in 1963 and, while there was no doubt that a laden four-cylinder Jeep Truck was underpowered, many of the rural customers for these vehicles had little interest in high-speed work and were more concerned with the reliability which the Hurricane engine certainly offered.

Nevertheless, sales of the Trucks were sinking in the early 1950s, exactly like those of the Station Wagons, and there can be little doubt that the model would have died a much earlier death if it had not been offered with the Super Hurricane six-cylinder engine which came as part of the deal with Kaiser in 1954. That engine was also available until the end of production, and it became the majority choice from the moment of its introduction.

Jeep Trucks were strictly workhorse vehicles, lacking both the glamour of the Station Wagons and the ready manoeuvrability of the short-wheelbase CJ models. Nevertheless, their sales contributed greatly to the profits of Willys Overland and, later, Kaiser-Willys, and their importance in the Jeep story is too often overlooked.

Even Trucks got the two-tone treatment in the early 1960s. This one shows the colour split also used on Utility Wagons between 1960 and 1963.

The Jeepster

It was Brooks Stevens who put forward the idea of the Jeepster as a postwar model, and his suggestion was made as early as 1944. Departed Willys-Overland President Joseph W Frazer had already coined the name of Jeepster for use on an abandoned convertible car project, and Stevens' concept of a sporty phaeton model like those popular in the 1930s was finally carried through to production in 1948. Stevens' original 1944 sketches suggested full-width rear bodywork similar to the lower part of the Station Wagon he had already designed, but by the time production started, the Jeep Truck had also become available and the new Willys-Overland management wanted to use that model's rear fenders and a more squared-off rear body. In the event, the fenders were slightly modified through the addition of a modesty panel at the top.

Jeepster production began on April 3, 1948, and the model was announced a month later with very little fanfare. While it was most certainly a distinctive vehicle, it never lived up to Willys-Overland's initial sales estimates of 50,000 units, and when production stopped in summer

The Jeepster was a stylish machine, though desperately underpowered for its pretensions. This is a 1948 example, with the side step found on original models.

1950 only just over one-fifth of that total had been built. Exactly what went wrong is hard to pinpoint, but there was no doubt that the Jeepster was always underpowered, just like its Station Wagon and Truck contemporaries. The real problem was that the lack of power was even more glaringly obvious on a vehicle with the Jeepster's sporting pretensions. It is also true that Willys showed little interest in developing the model, preferring to concentrate their efforts in the car field on the forthcoming Aero sedan, which was scheduled to appear in 1952. So the Jeepster quickly lost its appeal in the marketplace as the fashion-conscious buyers it was aimed at moved on to the next fad. One way or another, Jeepsters were built for two full seasons only, although there were several hundred unsold models in the showrooms by the end of that second season, and these were sold off as 1951 models.

The Jeepster or VJ model was based on the 104in two-wheel-drive chassis, with Planadyne independent front suspension. On 1948 and 1949 models its three-speed transmission came as standard with overdrive. All the 1948 models had the Go-Devil four-cylinder engine, but for 1949 the new Lightning six-cylinder was made optional, and quickly proved the more popular choice.

Nose styling was the same as on the contemporary Station Wagon, with the characteristic Jeep front flanked by squared-off fenders, and it was possible to order as an optional extra the stylish chromed ornamentation seen on the contemporary Station Sedan. Behind the bulkhead, however, the Jeepster had a unique two-door open body. This had a front bench seat with a one-third/two-thirds split, which folded forwards to give access to the rear bench, and on 1948 and 1949 models there was a step ahead of the rear wheel which allowed more athletic passengers to climb over the rear body sides and into their seats. The spare wheel was mounted, Continental-style, on the rear panel, and there was a folding soft-top with detachable side curtains to give a reasonable degree of weather protection. The canvas top on these early models, trimmed with red piping, was not known for its durability!

With sales picking up after the introduction of the six-cylinder model, Willys risked the expenditure of a mild facelift for the 1950 season. The flat, pressed grille was replaced by the new vee-grille introduced for 1950 on all members of the long-wheelbase Jeep family, the side step was deleted from the rear fender (mainly, it seems, because no-one ever used it) and the instrument panel was restyled. In addition, the soft-top was given a new counterbalancing system to make it easier to open and close, and new side curtains made of Vinylite took care of the earlier type's durability problem. As in other Jeep models, the Go-Devil four-cylinder engine was replaced by the more powerful Hurricane type and the Lightning was upgraded to 161ci F-head configuration. The 1950 models also dispensed with overdrive as standard equipment, although it remained an extra-cost option. In its place on that year's Jeepster Custom models came a radio, heater and various de luxe accessories.

Jeepsters were fashionable playthings of their time, and their popularity quickly waned. Without four-wheel drive (although several were later converted), they were not even appreciated by Jeep enthusiasts, but they are now recognized as a Milestone vehicle in the USA – the only Jeep vehicle to have been awarded that honour. They were also held in high enough esteem for the Jeepster name to be resurrected for a new range of vehicles in 1967 (see Chapter 5).

CHAPTER 7

The senior Jeeps (2)

Wagoneer, Cherokee and J-Truck

The replacements for the long-serving Station Wagons, Panel Deliveries and Jeep Trucks were long overdue by the time they were announced in November 1962 as 1963 models. Nevertheless, they did not disappoint buyer expectations, and went on to have an astonishingly long production life. Although the Panel Delivery lasted only until 1967 and the trucks were withdrawn in 1987, the final versions of the big Station Wagon models were not made until 1991. In the length of their production run, these models therefore exceeded the record set by the CJ-5.

By the time they were finally withdrawn, they were dinosaurs – bigger, more cumbersome and, above all, much thirstier than the fashionable vehicles of the day. Yet the Wagoneer represented an important landmark in the development of the modern 4x4 station wagon, for it was in so many ways the first proper dual-purpose 4x4 vehicle, suitable for use as an everyday car as well as for off-road driving.

These models spanned three major eras in the history of the Jeep marque, being developed during the period of Kaiser ownership, continuing right through the AMC period, and ending in the Chrysler period. It is worth noting that the change of manufacturer's name from Kaiser-Willys to the Kaiser-Jeep Corporation came about in 1963, the year after these models had been announced. Kaiser remained at the helm until 1970, when the Jeep Corporation was sold to AMC. AMC's ownership had a considerable impact on the further development of these models, and the AMC influence remained strong until

1987, when Jeep was sold to the Chrysler Corporation. Chrysler's influence was very much less marked; by that time, sales of the senior Jeeps had slowed right down, and they were old models which did not figure in Chrysler's grand plan for the marque. As a result, they were simply allowed to play out their time until a new model was ready in 1992.

Wagoneer chassis and engines
The basis of the range was a new low-profile chassis with a 110in wheelbase. With 6 inches more between axle centres, this inevitably made the vehicles bigger overall than the models they replaced. Yet this would not be the largest version of the chassis, which would also be stretched to various wheelbases up to 132 inches for the high-payload truck versions. When the suspension was modified for 1974 models in order to improve the ride, the wheelbase also changed (although the sheet metal of the body remained the same), and the basic wheelbase shrank to 108.7in. The chassis-frame was always of channel-section steel, but the 1976 models brought a stronger frame with partly-boxed side rails, and this remained until the end of production.

Most models had traditional leaf-spring suspension all round, but the two-wheel-drive models available from 1963 to 1967 had an interesting independent front suspension, which was also available to order on the 4x4 types of the period. Designed by A C Sampietro, who had taken over as Chief Engineer when Barney Roos retired in 1954, this used a single-pivot swing-axle layout, similar to that at the rear of

The original 1963 Wagoneer looked more like a conventional car-based station wagon than its boxy, van-like predecessors.

contemporary Mercedes-Benz cars. The two halves of the axle pivoted in a vertical plane along the centre-line of the car, and in theory steering knuckles prevented unwelcome camber changes. There were short upper A-arms, and springing was by longitudinal torsion bars, one running rearwards from each axle half. Unfortunately, camber change was not as well controlled as Willys had hoped, and so the independent front suspension system was dropped after a few years. Even the all-leaf spring suspension evolved over the years, as efforts were made to improve ride comfort. Longer front springs with paired rather than multi-leaf configuration were introduced for 1974, while 1976 brought asymmetrical rear springs and modified front springs giving longer wheel travel. At the same time, a new heavy-duty spring option became available for buyers whose priorities lay less in a comfortable ride than in load lugging or off-road work, while an anti-roll bar became optional on the front axle.

It was no surprise to find drum brakes on all four wheels when the Wagoneers were introduced. Yet these were rather marginal for vehicles of this weight and potential performance, even with the optional power assistance, so

from mid-1967 front wheel disc brakes became optional. They always came with power assistance. Yet even this was not a wholly foolproof system – particularly when the Wagoneer was carrying a heavy load in the back. Low-drag calipers were introduced on 1981 models, and lightweight discs and calipers arrived for 1990.

The steering was always a recirculating-ball system, and the first Wagoneers were notorious for their huge turning circles, not reduced until the new Dana 44 front axle was fitted to 1974 and later models. Power assistance was optional at first and later became standard, but it was always one of the weaker points of the Wagoneer, providing effortless steering at the cost of almost all feel. The Saginaw power steering introduced on 1974 models made little improvement. Like the brakes, the steering was modified for 1990, although the change simplified assembly and reduced weight without doing anything to improve feedback from wheels to driver.

The Wagoneers were big vehicles, and their size demanded powerful engines. So the senior Jeeps were always available with larger-capacity engines than could be had in the smaller and lighter CJs, although some engines were shared between the ranges. The first Wagoneer engine was not shared with the CJs, however. This was the Tornado OHC six-cylinder, which had been previewed briefly in the final examples of the old 104in wheelbase Station Wagons. Developed largely for the new model range, but with the Brazilian-built Willys sedans in mind as well, it had a 230ci (3.77-litre) capacity and used an efficient, modern overhead-camshaft design to give some 155bhp – although Kaiser-Jeep took the unusual step of expressing its output in nett figures of 140bhp. Even then, it was nearly twice as powerful as the four-cylinder which powered the CJ models.

The Tornado engine was really an overhead-camshaft conversion of the old Lightning six-cylinder, masterminded by Chief Engineer Sampietro. It featured the traditional Willys long stroke of 4.38in (shared with the Go-Devil and Hurricane fours, and with the Lightning six), but had a narrower bore. Technically, the engine was advanced for its time, featuring not only the overhead camshaft, but also a

The Super Wagoneer was introduced as an upmarket variant for 1966, the year when this new full-width grille was standardized.

cylinder head made of aluminium alloy with a water-heated manifold, crossflow porting for greater efficiency, spheroidal combustion chambers and lightweight valve gear.

Nevertheless, the Tornado engine lasted only until 1965 in the senior Jeeps, being relegated thereafter to the Willys sedans built in Brazil. It was replaced for the 1966 season by two new engines, bought in from Rambler (which would later transform itself into AMC, the company which in 1970 would buy the Jeep marque). The first of these was a direct replacement for the Tornado and was a 232ci (3.8-litre) six-cylinder which had been introduced in 1963 for the 1964 season. With 145bhp, it was even more powerful than the superseded Tornado, and it came with a formidable reputation for reliability. The second engine which Jeep took on was a much more powerful 327ci (5.4-litre) V8 known as the Vigilante, a 250bhp motor with a proven service record dating back to 1956. This became the extra-cost option in the senior Jeeps, and gave the heavy Wagoneer a good 90mph maximum speed.

The bought-in V8 could only be a short-term solution,

however, as it was already near the end of its production life. It disappeared from Rambler and AMC models in the middle of 1966, and lasted just a year longer as an optional motor in the senior Jeeps, although it lingered on for a further year in uprated 270bhp form as the power unit for the low-volume top-of-the-range Super Wagoneer until the end of the 1968 season. Jeep looked around for a replacement, and struck a deal with Buick to use their brand-new 350ci (5.7-litre) V8 from mid-1967, which was only marginally less powerful with 230bhp. This remained the optional engine alongside the AMC 232ci six-cylinder until AMC bought the Jeep marque and replaced all the bought-in engines with its own power units.

The new range of AMC engines was introduced in 1972 for the 1973 model-year and consisted of a six-cylinder as standard and a pair of optional V8s. The six-cylinder was no longer the 232ci type, but rather its long-stroke 258ci (4.2-litre) relative, which also became optional in CJ models and the Commando at the same time. The change had been brought about because new exhaust emissions regulations in

The dual-purpose nature of the Wagoneer is shown in this publicity picture of a 1970 model, supposedly serving on a construction site.

the USA, and a switch to unleaded petrol in 1971, had caused power outputs to drop dramatically right across the American motor industry, and extra swept volume was the simplest way of countering some of their effect. Even so, the engine's 110bhp was a lot less than the 232ci engine had offered, and Wagoneer buyers who wanted livelier acceleration and higher cruising speeds had to go for one of the V8s.

The two V8s had capacities of 304ci (5 litres) and 360ci (5.9 litres), and outputs of 150bhp and 175bhp respectively. Once again, these figures sound tame alongside the massive power outputs of the Rambler 327 and Buick 350 V8s of the previous decade. However, the Wagoneers powered by AMC's two V8s were nowhere near as underpowered as their paper specifications would suggest – although like many engines of the time, they were prone to some irritating rather than serious maladies caused by the emissions control

equipment they had to carry.

In any case it would not be long before AMC decided to put the power back into the big Jeeps. Coinciding with the introduction of the new and sportier Cherokee model on the Wagoneer line in 1974, the 360 V8 became available with a four-barrel carburettor as well as in original two-barrel tune, and an even bigger 401ci (6.6-litre) V8 became the top-of-the-range option. This engine had first appeared in 1971-model AMC cars, and was a long-stroke derivative of the company's 390ci V8 which had been introduced on 1968 models. Once again, it was a well-tried and reliable motor, and with 215bhp it put back into the Wagoneer and Cherokee models most of the performance which had been missing since the end of the Kaiser era.

Between 1974 and 1979, therefore, there were four engine options for the senior Jeeps. Beginning with the 258ci six-cylinder which was standard, they went on up through 360 two-barrel V8 and 360 four-barrel V8 to the range-topping 401 V8. This latter even became available as an option in Jeep Trucks from 1976, but after the second oil crisis in 1979 AMC decided it would be better to drop this gas-guzzling engine altogether, and the two-barrel 360 V8 became the top option on 1980 models.

As exhaust emissions regulations grew tighter during the 1980s, so the power of the surviving engines was gradually stifled. The 258 six was thoroughly overhauled for 1981 to save 90lb in weight and give better driveability and fuel economy, but it lasted only until 1986, leaving the 144bhp two-barrel 360 V8 as the only Grand Wagoneer engine for 1987. By the time the last of these big Jeeps was built four years later, the latest 241ci (4-litre) injected six-cylinder engine in the XJ Cherokee range was giving vastly better power and performance figures, but slow sales had dissuaded Chrysler from devoting the time and effort to put it into the ageing Wagoneer range.

Wagoneer transmissions
The first Wagoneers could be bought with either rear-wheel-drive or four-wheel-drive transmissions, although it soon became clear to Kaiser that the real appeal of these big station wagons lay in the extra traction provided by four-

wheel drive, and so the 4x2 models ceased production in 1965. The standard gearbox had only three forward speeds before 1980, although there were different varieties: 4x2 models had all-synchromesh gearboxes while 4x4s had no synchromesh on bottom gear before 1973. The 4x2 models could also be had with an optional overdrive.

Heavy-duty four-speed gearboxes became optional in the mid-1960s, and these featured an ultra-low (6.32:1) first gear, which was really too low for everyday road use and was generally ordered only when the Wagoneer was used for towing a heavy trailer or caravan, or for difficult off-road work. A lighter-duty all-synchromesh four-speed gearbox was standardized on 1980 and 1981 models, but with the 1982 Wagoneers came a five-speed type with an overdrive fifth gear designed to promote better fuel economy at cruising speeds.

However, perhaps the most notable transmission in the Wagoneers was a three-speed automatic, which was optional from the beginning. It came without a low range of gears (until 1973), because the shift into low ratio was by

sliding spur gears, which demanded a manual clutch. The Wagoneer was the first series-production sport-utility vehicle to have an automatic gearbox and this, like so many other items of Jeep hardware at the time, was a bought-in component. Between 1963 and 1965, a three-speed Borg-Warner gearbox was used, but Jeep then changed to the General Motors Turbo-Hydramatic 400. Also a three-speed type, this gearbox was acknowledged to be the best automatic transmission then on the market, and was strong enough to withstand all the torque which the Jeep engines could throw at it – and it was smooth enough in operation to be chosen a few years later as the standard transmission for Rolls-Royce and Bentley cars. The Turbo-Hydramatic gave way to a Chrysler Torque-Flite for 1981 and this remained available until the end of Wagoneer production, latterly becoming the preferred choice of the elderly and conservative buyers who accounted for the majority of Wagoneer sales.

All the 4x4 Wagoneers with manual transmissions came with a transfer gearbox, which provided crawler gears for

Bench front seats made the Wagoneer into a spacious six-seater. A notable design feature was the centrally-placed glove locker - accessible to driver and passenger alike.

rough-terrain work and performed the function of dividing the drive between front and rear axles. Between 1963 and 1973, the transfer box was a Dana Model 20 – new with the Wagoneer in November 1962 – which broke new ground with its through-drive configuration. The box had no high range of gears; for normal road use, the drive simply went straight through the box to the rear axle, bypassing the extra gears and thus eliminating the gear whine so characteristic of dual-range transfer boxes. Two-wheel drive was available in high range (and manually lockable freewheeling hubs were available to reduce wear in the front drivetrain components); four-wheel drive could also be had in high range for rough-terrain work (although there was no centre differential to prevent axle wind-up, so this was not suitable for prolonged road use); and four-wheel drive was automatically engaged when low range in the transfer box was selected.

A new permanent four-wheel drive system arrived on 1973 models with automatic transmission and was standardized with manual transmission a year later. This was known as Quadra-Trac, and its advantage was to allow four-wheel drive to be used on the road and thus improve both handling and traction. It consisted of a chain-driven single-speed transfer gearbox which divided the drive between front and rear wheels by means of a central differential incorporating a cone clutch which gave power to the wheels according to demand. In an emergency, the central differential could be locked by means of a switch hidden in the Wagoneer's glovebox. However, with Quadra-Trac, a second set of crawler gears was an extra-cost option, which came in the shape of an additional two-range gearbox bolted to the back of the main transmission.

Quadra-Trac lasted until 1979, when it was dropped in the wake of the second oil crisis. Public sensitivity to the cost of fuel and Government insistence on forthcoming fuel saving measures persuaded Jeep to abandon the system because there was no doubt that permanent four-wheel drive used more fuel than a selectable system. So for 1980 the Wagoneers were fitted with Chrysler's New Process 208 two-speed transfer gearbox, which brought a welcome 2.61:1 low ratio to offset the effect of taller overall gearing

introduced to improve fuel consumption. The Chrysler transfer box introduced Selec-Trac, which included a torque-biasing viscous-coupled central differential so that four-wheel drive could be used on the road. The central differential, of course, could be locked as well, while drive to the front axle could be disconnected by means of a vacuum clutch to improve fuel economy.

Wagoneer and Panel Delivery bodies
Jeep exploited its new chassis and body combination to the very hilt, using it as the basis of station wagons with both two and four doors, a Panel Delivery van and a series of small trucks. Within the basic body-and-chassis combinations, powertrain and other options created a bewildering array of possible specifications, and of course special editions widened the field even further.

Kaiser entrusted the styling of the Wagoneer to Brooks Stevens Associates, of Milwaukee, the company which had been responsible for the earlier Station Wagons. The result was a first of its kind as the vehicle had been drawn up to resemble as closely as possible the typical car-derived station wagon of the time. It was bigger and perhaps boxier, but there was no doubt that it was radically different from the old Jeep Station Wagon, being lower and sleeker in appearance. Both two-door and four-door Wagoneers were offered at first, although the four-door proved by far the more popular and the two-door was dropped in 1965. This two-door body was also used for the Panel Delivery van, introduced alongside the Wagoneers in 1962 and featuring metal panels instead of windows in the sides of its van body. Slow sales caused the Panel Delivery to cease production in 1967, however.

The first Wagoneers and all the Panel Deliverys had a large chromed rectangular grille in the centre of the front panel, but this disappeared when the new engines arrived on 1966 models, to be replaced by a full-width grille which made the vehicle look lower, wider and more car-like from the front. A new grille with horizontal bars instead of the earlier 'toothy' appearance and with running lights at the corners was introduced for 1971, and gave way to a hatched grille on 1974 models. This remained unaltered until 1980,

The final Grand Wagoneers were simply big luxury barges. This is a 1989 model.

when a new vertical-bar grille incorporating rectangular headlamps was fitted. Halogen lamps were added for 1982, and the final grille was introduced on 1986 models, retaining the rectangular lamps but this time with horizontal bars. Tail-lights were square and plain on the earliest models, but took on chromed frames on later types and from 1974 were changed for elongated, vertical units.

A Wagoneer Custom with de luxe equipment was available from the beginning, and came with such items as carpets, a chromed grille and bright trim on the dashboard, round the windows and on the wheels. Seats on the standard models were upholstered in vinyl with fabric inserts, but could be foam-padded to order, and power operation for the tailgate glass was another option. This was just a beginning, however. As the Wagoneer became accepted as an alternative to a car, so the customers demanded more and more luxury and convenience items – so Kaiser-Jeep provided them.

With the 1965 models came the first of the special-edition Wagoneers. This was known as the Super Wagoneer

and lasted until 1968 (when it was relegated to an option package). As its name suggests, it was a Wagoneer loaded with a large selection of the extras then available, plus a few unique to the model. The Super Wagoneer was recognizable by its two-tone finish and special spoked wheel covers. Inside, it featured de luxe trim with bucket front seats, a tilt steering column and a sporty floor-mounted gearshift lever in place of the regular column shift. All Super Wagoneers came with the four-barrel 327 V8 engine, and all of them had four-wheel drive.

For 1974, the new Cherokee model was introduced, with a two-door version of the Wagoneer body and a more sporting demeanour. So from this date, the Wagoneer was repositioned in the luxury market, and began to move gradually into the role of elder statesman. As such, it appealed to older buyers who demanded more and more luxury and convenience features. There was a Wagoneer Custom in 1976, and from 1978 a special edition package turned the basic model into a Wagoneer Limited, which was easily identified by the fake wood panels on its flanks and –

1986 models brought a new instrument panel and heater controls, while 1988's innovation was an electric sunroof. The 1989 model-year introduced an overhead console, remote central locking and a rear wash-wipe as standard. But all that Jeep could muster for the Grand Wagoneer's final season was some new colours.

The Cherokee

General Motors introduced the Chevrolet Blazer and GMC Jimmy in 1969, when these new and stylish sport-utility models quickly made the Wagoneer look rather staid and started to eat away at its sales. So when AMC took over the Jeep marque at the beginning of the new decade, they determined to do something about the problem. The result arrived as a 1974 model, and was neither more nor less than a reworked two-door station wagon body with a number of extras to give it a more sporting appeal. AMC called it the Jeep Cherokee, and it was a massive success, elevating the 10-year-old design into the front ranks of sport-utility models. Over the 10 years of its production, the Cherokee shared its mechanical development with the Wagoneer, but it remained a quite distinctive model to the end.

The Cherokee was developed as a credible off-roader,

The Cherokee was introduced in 1974 as a sporty two-door variant of the senior Jeep line and became a big success.

not surprisingly – by 'Limited' nameplates. Air conditioning, cruise control, thick carpeting and an AM/FM radio with built-in CB were among the other features which made this model a massive success. For 1981, the Wagoneer range was realigned with three models on offer – Custom, Brougham and Limited – and a new air dam was added under the front bumper. Then with the introduction of a Wagoneer Limited based on the new XJ models for 1984, the older model moved up yet another rung to become a Grand Wagoneer, still with fake wood side panels – and so it remained until the end.

Nevertheless, its development was not yet over, and the remaining seven years of Grand Wagoneer production saw a number of improvements, mainly to the model's luxury and convenience equipment. There were gold-coloured wheel trim inserts for 1985, plus interior changes allowing three belted passengers to be carried on the front bench seat. The

The 1974 Cherokee S came with these tasty alloy wheels and a roof rack as standard.

The wide-track Cherokee Chief added a businesslike appearance to its off-road credentials. This is a 1981 model.

while the Wagoneer became progressively more car-like and refined. Although the base engine was the 258ci six-cylinder, the model really came into its own when equipped with the 360 or 401 V8 engines. The shape of the rear side windows helped to give the vehicle a lean profile, a white roof on all models proved distinctive, and the front had an aggressive demeanour from its large chromed grille with vertical slats, which looked more like teeth. This had in fact been borrowed from the truck line. Dished six-spoke alloy wheels helped to distinguish the model further from the Wagoneer, and pricing also helped the Cherokee to establish its own niche.

A late 1970s four-door Cherokee Chief, with added running lights on the roof.

The workhorse of the Second World War has been a popular collector's item for many years. Here are three preserved UK-registered Jeeps on parade, the one closest to the camera featuring the early welded iron slatted grille.

This Colorado-registered CJ-2A has an aftermarket hardtop and has been subtly updated. The A-frame on the front bumper allows it to be towed at speeds it could never achieve under its own power!

In the beginning, the Cherokee came in two versions, a standard model and a Cherokee S equipped with such items as extra chrome, embossed vinyl trim, accent decals on the sides, a roof rack and forged aluminium alloy wheels. These were followed by a Cherokee Chief, announced in January 1975, but in practice not available until several months after that. This came with special wide-track axles and eight-spoke wheels with the latest wide off-road tyres. There were fender extensions to cover these, and the Chief package also included flat black striping with the name on rocker panels and tailgate, extra chrome mouldings, chrome bumpers and a padded sports steering wheel. The so-called Levi's upholstery was optional. In later years, the details of the Chief package varied, but it was always a sporty, showy, wide-track variant of the Cherokee.

From 1977, in an interesting exploitation of available resources, AMC announced a four-door Cherokee alongside the two-door model. This used the Wagoneer's body, but of course with clear Cherokee identification from items such as the grille, wheels and side decals. It failed to look as sporty as the two-door model, but it found enough buyers to keep AMC happy. Then from 1979, the smooth-ride suspension also introduced on the Wagoneer was made available, although not on the wide-track models.

That same year brought an export-only Cherokee Limited, which was a luxury edition of the two-door model. It had air conditioning, leather upholstery, thick carpets and an AM/FM stereo radio among its standard features. Automatic transmission and power-assisted steering were also in the specification, and the model wore eight-spoke wheels and a new grille with narrow horizontal bars. Back home, the top Cherokee trim option from 1980 was the Laredo package, and for 1981 the options included a removable smoked glass sunroof, a roller blind for the rear load space, and double front dampers on the sporty wide-track models. The final Cherokees were built in 1983, when the model was withdrawn to make way for the new downsized XJ range. That AMC chose to use the Cherokee name for their important new models was an indication of the impact which the original had made.

This late 1960s Gladiator J-3000 has the original frontal styling.

The Gladiators and J-series Trucks

Kaiser-Jeep introduced Truck derivatives of the Wagoneer at the same time as the parent model in November 1962, and between then and 1969 these were known as Gladiator models. They came initially as a J-200 with 120in wheelbase and 7ft cargo box, and as a J-300 with 126in wheelbase and 8ft cargo box. Designations changed to J-2000 and J-3000 when new engines arrived for 1966, and for 1969 the wheelbase of the J-3000 was increased to 132in. Beginning with the 1970 models, the Gladiator name was dropped and the models were simply known as J-series Trucks. AMC also introduced a heavy-duty J-4000 range on the long wheelbase in 1972. Payload options had always been either ½-ton or ¾-ton, but for 1973 the long-wheelbase ¾-ton trucks could be fitted with a heavy-duty suspension option to give them a GVW rating of 8,000lb.

Wheelbase sizes and designations changed when the new front suspension arrived on 1974 models, and the Trucks then came as J-10s and J-20s with wheelbases of 118.7in and 130.7in. The shorter wheelbase was discontinued after 1984, and from 1985 on the J-10 and J-20 designations

A late-1970s J-20 showing the peaked roof. The J-series Trucks are a rare sight in the UK.

The separate rear fenders of the Sportside option gave this French-registered J-10 a new and tougher appearance.

were used to indicate engine options (six-cylinder and V8, respectively) on the 130.7in-wheelbase chassis. However, by this time, sales of these elderly trucks were only moderate, so a month after Chrysler took over in 1987 they were dropped from production to avoid in-house competition with Chrysler's own range of Dodge trucks.

From the beginning, the standard bodies were Townside pick-ups or stake-sides, and buyers were mostly farmers and other rural users. A stepside pick-up was introduced under the Thriftside name, but disappeared under AMC in 1973. However, when the more sporty trucks fielded by Dodge, Ford and Chevrolet in the early 1970s began to damage J-series truck sales, Toledo hit back with the sporty Honcho (1976-84) and Golden Eagle (1978) models, and for 1981 re-introduced a stepside body under the Sportside name on J-10 Trucks only. This barrage of new models gave the J-series Trucks a new image and was successful with a new breed of younger buyer. Meanwhile, the biggest models with heavy-payload options remained favourites with those who equipped them with demountable camper bodies.

The CJ-2A marked the start of the Jeep's long and eventful life as a versatile civilian product, and more than 40 years on the YJ Wrangler, in the background, is a reminder that the basic concept of the original remains good.

Chrome featured heavily on the CJ-7 Laredo of the early 1980s. The heavily dished wheels and fat tyres make an interesting contrast with the anaemic looking rubber on the light truck in the background.

The first Gladiator models had the 140bhp Tornado six-cylinder engine, but for 1966 they switched to the 232ci six-cylinder with the Dauntless 350ci V8 as an option. The 1970s brought AMC and the 258ci six-cylinder as the entry-level engine, with the 304ci and 360ci V8s as options. The two-barrel 360 was standard on J-4000 models with the 7,000lb and 8,000lb payload options from the 1972 season onwards; the four-barrel 360 was an option from the 1976 model-year, and even the 401ci V8 could be had from 1976 to 1979. However, the 258ci six-cylinder was the base engine from 1980 on, with the 360 optional except in California because it could not meet that state's tight emissions control standards.

Both four-wheel-drive and rear-wheel-drive models were available in the beginning, but the 4x2 models had a leaf-sprung beam front axle instead of the swinging axles of the 4x2 Wagoneers. All models had 4x4 transmission by the end of the 1960s. The first vehicles had a three-speed gearbox as standard, but the T-98A heavy-duty four-speed arrived during the later 1960s. Automatic transmission with the obligatory Quadra-Trac permanent four-wheel drive became available in 1973, but was discontinued for 1980, as on the Wagoneer and Cherokee models. Then 1982 J-series Trucks were the first with the combination of automatic transmission and six-cylinder (258ci) engine. From 1983, Australian-built examples (which had special CJ-style front panels with rectangular headlamps in the wing fronts) could have a 3.25-litre six-cylinder Nissan SD33 diesel engine with 94bhp and 159lb.ft of torque, although this was not available for other markets.

Although the final 1987 J-series trucks were immediately recognizable as descendants of the original 1963 Gladiators, a number of details had changed over the intervening decade and a half. The original rectangular grille design had remained until 1969, when it was replaced by a full-width chromed type with vertical slats. A further change came on 1980 models, which had a black plastic grille of vertical slats with a chromed frame, and then 1981 and later models had an all-chromed version of the same design. Meanwhile, tail-lamps had changed for 1973, when the truck bed gained double-skinned sidewalls. The

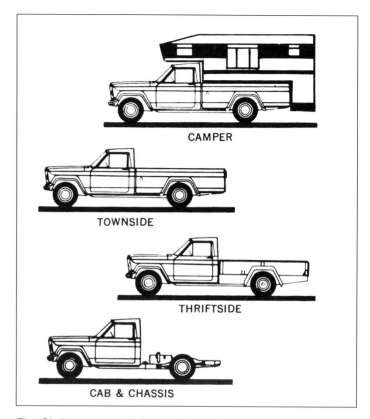

CAMPER

TOWNSIDE

THRIFTSIDE

CAB & CHASSIS

The Gladiator came in four basic versions, as shown here. The Sportside style of the 1980s was different yet again.

1979 models had introduced a one-piece aluminium front bumper with optional black rubber overriders, and 1981 models were the first to have a rounded front to the cab roof in place of the characteristic peaked type. These 1981 models also brought new suspension, which lowered the whole vehicle by 1.25 inches.

Option packages were also available from the early days. The 1966 model-year, for example, brought a Safety Package of seat belts, padded dash and dual-circuit brakes.

The J-4800 version of the J-4000 132in-wheelbase Truck was designed for a GVW of 8,000lb, of which 4,061lb were payload. This version was a favourite as the basis of demountable campers such as the one seen here.

Truck instrumentation was broadly similar to that of contemporary Wagoneers.

But it was under AMC that options really became an important part of Jeep Truck marketing, as equipment levels were fine-tuned to suit the emerging trend towards fashionable rather than purely utilitarian trucks. AMC kicked off with the 1975 Pioneer luxury package, consisting on the outside of fake wood trim, a chromed front bumper, bright window frames and wheel covers; inside, there was more fake wood on the instrument panel, pleated fabric seats and deep pile carpets; and the finishing touch was dual horns.

The sporty Honcho package arrived in December 1976 on both wheelbases. It featured large side decals with the Honcho name, a chromed front bumper and rear step bumper, styled steel wheels with Goodyear Tracker tyres and various interior enhancements. There was also a rollover bar behind the cab. A year later came the Golden Eagle package, with the huge spread-eagle on the hood panel, additional side decals, gold anodized wheels, the

A Jeep Truck equipped with a flat-bed body preserved in the UK. Trucks were built on an extended 118in-wheelbase chassis and remained in production from 1947 to 1963, thanks to the Kaiser takeover in 1954, which led to some urgently needed extra power being provided by the Super Hurricane six-cylinder engine.

This low-angle shot of a French-registered J10 truck emphasises the aggressive styling which was characteristic of the later J-series vehicles.

A 1993-registered Jeep Wrangler 4.0 Limited with the latest roll-over hoop, full-height doors and light clusters outboard of the rectangular headlamps, which would shortly give way to round units.

Later Trucks took on styling accessories to compete in the sporty truck market of the 1970s. This is the 1978-model Honcho.

J-series Trucks were often adapted to special purposes. This J-20 is one of a pair converted to three-axle layout and fitted with rescue tender bodywork by Fulton and Wylie for the Staffordshire Fire and Rescue Service in Britain. They were joined in 1987 by a third J-20, this time bodied by Dennis.

chromed front bumper, rear step bumper and a black brush guard. Cibie high-intensity driving lamps were also installed (by Jeep dealers) on the rollover bar. A 10-4 option brought a CB radio, among other items. A Custom package was available from 1978 on the high-payload J-20 models, which were denied the Honcho and Golden Eagle options.

By the time of their demise in 1987, the J-series Trucks could be had with such options as electric windows, central locking and electrically-adjusted mirrors. They came with comfortable bucket seats in place of the original three-abreast bench, and they had the same three-dial instrumentation (introduced in 1973) as the Wagoneers and Cherokees. That these items and the sporty special-edition packages should have been introduced on vehicles designed as utilitarian load-carriers is a clear indication of the way the light truck market in the USA had evolved over a decade and a half.

CHAPTER 8

The XJ range

Cherokee, Wagoneer Limited and Comanche

It was during 1978 that the Jeep engineers under AMC's Roy Lunn started work on design concepts for a range of models to replace the existing Cherokee, Wagoneer and their truck derivatives. They called their new design the XJ (for eXperimental Jeep), because some of the engineering concepts it embodied were quite new to the Jeep marque. Perhaps most important was that the new model was to feel much more car-like than the existing senior Jeeps – even though they, many years earlier, had been several steps closer to conventional station wagon design than their truck-like predecessors.

At this stage, AMC was taking a strong interest in the possibilities of four-wheel drive for road cars. The 1980 model-year brought the new Eagle line (later developed into a separate marque), which added a 4x4 drivetrain to the AMC Concord sedan in order to improve roadholding and traction rather than to give it any serious off-road potential. In order to simplify the four-wheel drive system for car drivers who were not used to the extra levers associated with off-road vehicles, a new control system was developed. This allowed a fuel-saving freewheel mode for the front wheels to be selected by pressing a button on the dashboard, and the system was known as Select-Drive. Its simplicity and the positive response it elicited from buyers persuaded AMC that this was the way to go with four-wheel drive systems on Jeeps as well.

Meanwhile, two further events had an impact on the development of the new XJ range. The first was the purchase of a 46.4% shareholding in AMC by the French Renault company during 1979. This brought a new and more European orientation, as well as welcome additional funding at a time when sales of AMC's mainstream products were tumbling. The second was the oil crisis of that year, which once again focused the attention of the world's motor manufacturers on the cost of fuel and in consequence the need to make vehicles as fuel-efficient as possible.

Under Renault (who acquired a controlling interest in AMC during 1982 and would hold it until 1987), the existing ideas for the XJ range were reviewed in the light of the new need for more fuel-efficient vehicles. The original project was in effect scrapped, although much of its engineering and styling was retained. The second-stage XJ project was subject to a very strong European influence, and not only from Renault as the primary source of finance – although it may have been Renault who decreed that all nuts and bolts would be of metric sizes for the first time on a Jeep. As the 1980s dawned, European cars were becoming increasingly popular in the USA because of their fuel economy, and it was very clear to American motor industry executives that future domestic cars would have to be as small as the European models with which they would inevitably compete.

Renault also appear to have encouraged Jeep to think in terms of much larger-scale production than before. The market for sport-utility vehicles was beginning to take off in Europe, and through the Renault network Jeep would have an access to this market which was unprecedented in their

What a difference a wheel makes . . .
this right-hand-drive Cherokee 4.0 Sport
has stylish five-spokes . . .

. . . while this later model, also right-hand-
drive, has the wheels associated with the
2.5-litre engine.

Softer, more rounded styling characterized the revised front ends of 1998 models, aiming to compete in the increasingly fashion-conscious 4x4 market.

The 1998 Cherokees also had a new-style tailgate, extending the rounder, less angular look to the rear as well. This is a right-hand-drive 4.0-litre Limited.

The two-door Cherokee Sport model was intended to appeal to younger buyers. This 1989 model had the 4-litre engine and a five-speed manual gearbox.

history. Renault were building versions of their cars in America for the US market, and the *quid pro quo* was that AMC (primarily in the shape of Jeep) would be able to sell their products in Europe. So to allow for this increased production, and to ensure that it was carried out as efficiently as possible, Renault pumped $250 million into a major renovation of the Jeep plant at Toledo. This enabled Jeep to plan for a first-year output of 40,000 XJ models when production began in June 1983.

The key to the revised XJ project was downsizing, the buzz-word which went around the American motor industry in the early 1980s as manufacturers struggled to reconcile the conflicting demands of cleaner exhausts and greater fuel economy. However, even though size was generally the focus of attention, the real problem for fuel economy lay in weight. So the Jeep engineers sought every possible way of reducing the weight of the XJ models without losing too much of the size and spaciousness which had been so much appreciated in the existing Wagoneer and Cherokee lines. Their search led to the radical decision to abandon the

traditional Jeep body-on-frame construction, and to use unitary construction for the XJ range.

In this, they were able to draw on AMC's own experience with unitary construction in sedans, and on Renault's even longer experience in the same field. In the 4x4 world, however, it was revolutionary. The only regular-production 4x4s with unitary construction up to this time had been small military runabouts (like the Mighty Mite and Ford MUTT) and the Russian-built Lada Niva. No manufacturer had ever attempted to build such a large unitary body for a 4x4 vehicle which would be subjected to the stresses and strains of off-road driving. While the XJ was a noble effort, there was no doubt that the unitary body of early examples did twist to a noticeable extent in extreme conditions.

Managing without a separate chassis-frame saved a lot of weight, but the Jeep engineers were determined to save even more by making their new vehicle physically smaller than the one it would replace. There was also a marketing influence here; even if the lighter unitary construction *would* save enough weight to make the XJ a class-leader in fuel economy, it was likely to be perceived as old-fashioned and thirsty alongside the downsized models which were bound to come from other manufacturers. Therefore, the new model had to be smaller than the old.

So the Jeep engineers settled on a wheelbase of 101.4in, which was just over 7in shorter than that of the existing senior Jeeps. They slimmed the body down by 6in, and by trimming the front and rear overhangs made their new vehicle an incredible 21in shorter than the models it would replace. The result was a saving of 1,000lb in weight as compared to the older models, for the loss – according to Jeep – of only 10% in interior space.

However, there was no doubt that the XJ felt a lot smaller inside than the old J-series station wagons. Perhaps most noticeable was the low roofline, which had been engineered partly as a way of minimizing size and weight, but also of making the styling more car-like. As far as appearance was concerned, the stylists under AMC's Dick Teague appeared to have taken the strong-selling Volvo estate car as their benchmark, and there was no doubt that the XJ did resemble that vehicle in its general proportions.

Suspension and drivetrain

When the new Jeep Cherokee and Wagoneer Limited models were announced in September 1983, a few months after the assembly lines had started rolling, there was more than just their unitary construction to astonish onlookers. They came with a coil-sprung front axle, which represented a first for the Jeep marque, although coil-spring suspension was not new to off-road vehicles in general. The Range Rover, for example, had featured coil springs all round since 1970, and the little Lada had had them since 1978.

However, Jeep had not specified a coil-sprung front end simply to follow the trend. One reason was that it gave better ride and handling, and was thus in keeping with the objectives of the new XJ. But a second and perhaps more important reason was associated with the packaging of the new vehicle. It was impossible to position the front axle

In the middle of the range, the two-door shell was also available as a Cherokee Limited . . .

close to the nose of the vehicle when leaf springs were used because their location demanded a certain amount of space ahead of the axle. Yet a short front overhang lowered the vehicle's sprung weight and also gave a better angle of approach for off-road work. The only way of achieving this desirable short overhang was by using coil springs instead of leaf springs.

Coil springs, of course, only act as a springing medium, whereas leaf springs also locate the axle, so a new axle location system was developed for the XJ. It had two unequal arms on each side, one above the other and not working in parallel. Jeep patented it and gave it the name of Quadra-Link. It acted in conjunction with a Panhard rod to give lateral location, and an anti-roll bar to prevent excessive lean in corners. At the rear, however, there was no need for any new solution, and the live rear axle was sprung and located in the traditional manner on multi-leaf springs. The dampers were canted to optimize space utilization as well as ride quality, and there was another anti-roll bar.

The axles were a Dana Model 30 at the front, and

AMC's own at the rear. The first XJs came with a 3.31:1 final-drive ratio as standard and a 3.73:1 option, but these ratios would change in later years. Steering was a recirculating-ball type made by General Motors' Saginaw division, and the power assistance, which was standard on more expensive XJ variants, could be bought as an option on the others. Brakes, meanwhile, featured ventilated discs on the front wheels and drums at the rear, and power assistance was standard on all models.

Transfer boxes in all models were lightweight two-speed types made by Chrysler's New Process division and already seen on other Jeep models from 1981. Cheaper XJ variants had the Command-Trac system, with a Model 207 transfer gearbox and manually lockable front hubs. The more expensive models had Selec-Trac (derived from the Eagle's Select-Drive system) with a viscous-coupled centre differential, which allowed four-wheel drive to be used on paved surfaces, and with the vacuum-operated freewheeling front hubs. Further up the drivetrain, the standard gearbox was a four-speed manual. A five-speed variant of this with the same ratios but an additional overdrive fifth speed was optional, and of course there was an automatic option in the shape of Chrysler's three-speed Model 904.

The 1984-model XJ range offered both a frugal four-cylinder and a modern six-cylinder engine. The four-cylinder was brand-new and was built by AMC, being derived from that company's long-serving in-line six. It had a capacity of 150 cubic inches and offered 105bhp and a sporting demeanour. There had been insufficient money to develop an all-new six-cylinder engine (although work was already under way on modernizing the existing AMC six), so the six-cylinder option in the XJ range was a 173ci V6 bought in from General Motors' Chevrolet division. This had first been seen in Chevrolet's 1980-model Citation, and it promised a smooth if unexciting 110bhp.

The models
The initial XJ range consisted of two-door and four-door Cherokees with black grilles, and four-door Wagoneers with bright grilles. Sporty Cherokee and staid Wagoneer also differed in their tail-lights, trim mouldings, wheels, interior design, interior trim and upholstery materials. The Cherokees could be ordered with Pioneer and Chief packages, and the Wagoneers came in Brougham or Limited forms, the latter with leather inside and fake wood outside. For 1985 a Laredo option was added to the Cherokee line, with special side decals and badges, bright finish for the grille, mouldings and door handles, and colour-keyed fender flares. Then Wagoneers took on a two-tier grille with stacked lamps for 1986 to reinforce the distinction between the two ranges.

Pioneer and Chief packages disappeared for 1989, and then for 1991 the Wagoneers were dropped and replaced by a Cherokee Briarwood. This had all the equipment seen on the last Wagoneers, including the fake wood trim, but it was positioned below the Limited in the price range. So by 1992, the range consisted of Cherokee Sport, Laredo, Briarwood and Limited. However, the arrival of the ZJ Grand Cherokee prompted a further realignment, and the range was retargeted at younger buyers for 1993 with a

More differences, this time on a 1989 Wagoneer Limited. It has the four-door body with adjustable roof rack, but grille, bumper and wheels are all different, and that fake wood on the sides was unique to the model at this stage.

99

This early 1990s four-door Cherokee Limited is broadly similar to the 1989 model, but note the protection panels on the lower flanks, and bumpers and decals which are different yet again.

three-model line-up of base, Sport and Country. In Europe, meanwhile, where a new sales push began in the early 1990s, the Cherokees had a simple hierarchy based on traditional Jeep names. They came as base, Sport or Limited models, although some importers created incremental models with different equipment levels; by 1995 in Britain, for example, there were Sport SE and Limited SE models as well.

Specification changes
The new models received an extraordinarily favourable reception, winning three American 4x4 of the Year awards in their first season and captivating customers. The V6 engine was undoubtedly disappointing, but AMC had their new 4-litre derivative of the old 258 six-cylinder ready for the 1987 season, and this replaced the Chevrolet engine in all models. The new 173bhp motor – later christened the Power-Tech Six – proved to be a superb piece of machinery, with a smooth power delivery, plenty of torque in the low and mid-ranges, and excellent fuel economy for

its size. It was closely related to the existing 2.5-litre four-cylinder which had been derived from the same original design.

Meanwhile, 1986 had brought a third engine option in the shape of a Renault-built turbodiesel. This was initially available for export only, put in a brief appearance in the USA on 1987 models, but did not prove popular and was therefore relegated to an export-only option again. Built in France and shipped out to Toledo for installation in XJ models, this engine was derived from the aluminium-block 2.1-litre diesel already seen in CJ Jeeps for export. The turbocharged version had been developed originally for the French company's 1982 R20 and R30 sedans and at a time when diesel engines were becoming popular in the USA. With just 82bhp, turbodiesel Cherokees lacked much of the sparkle of their bigger-engined brethren, but through-the-gears acceleration was adequate, thanks to the turbodiesel's good torque.

The 2.5-litre four-cylinder and 4-litre six-cylinder engines remained the staple powerplants of the range from now on,

The author drove this RHD Cherokee 4.0 Limited at an off-road demonstration day, and rated its engine as excellent, but its transmission controls over-complicated.

The high-output 4-litre engine in the XJ range was developed from the old 258ci AMC six-cylinder.

although power outputs varied over the years. The four-cylinder's two-barrel carburettor gave way to throttle-body injection for 1986, increasing power to 117bhp that year and to 121bhp for 1987. For 1988 the 4-litre went up to 177bhp, and then to 190bhp for 1991, at which time the four-cylinder took on the six-cylinder's sequential multi-point injection and went up to 130bhp.

The Renault 2.1-litre turbodiesel option was dropped for 1994, and the Cherokee was equipped instead with the very much more powerful VM HR494 Turbotronic engine, a 2.5-litre turbocharged indirect-injection type built in Italy and already used in the European-built Chrysler Voyager. Fitted with an intercooler as standard, this engine offered 116bhp at 4,000rpm and an impressive 207lb.ft of torque at 2,000rpm. To keep nitrogen oxide levels within the limits demanded by the latest exhaust emissions regulations, the Turbotronic engine was fitted with an EGR (Exhaust Gas Recirculation) system. This operated by means of a valve which intercepted and recycled the gasflow. The valve was modulated by an electronic control unit, which in turn

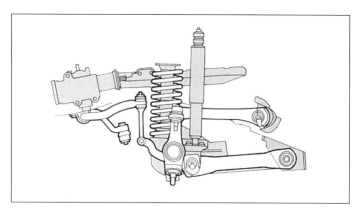

The front axle of the XJ model range featured coil springs and Quadra-Link location.

controlled the engine's thermodynamic cycle.

There were other important mechanical changes over the years. Two-wheel-drive Cherokees appeared in the middle of the 1985 model-year, creating a base model in the two-door bodyshell with the four-cylinder engine. From spring 1988, however, a 4-litre Cherokee Sport with the 4x4 drivetrain could be bought. Selec-Trac transmissions gained a shift-on-the-fly feature to bring them into line with the lesser Command-Trac types for 1985, and for 1986 a Trac-Lok limited-slip rear differential became optional. Selec-Trac also gained single-lever control for 1987.

The 1987 model-year introduced a new four-speed automatic transmission with electronic controls, Comfort and Power modes, and an overdrive top gear. This had been developed jointly by Aisin Seiki of Japan and Warner Gears in the USA, and came only with the six-cylinder engine until the end of 1993; 1994 models were the first to offer automatic transmission with the four-cylinder engine. Bendix had developed the four-wheel ABS braking system which became optional on six-cylinder models for 1989, and this scored a first on the domestic market because other vehicles in the Cherokee's class offered ABS on the rear wheels only. This valuable new safety aid later became available on other models as well.

Inside the 4.0-litre Limited, this was the new-for-1998 dashboard. The upholstery is leather, of course.

Interior features, too, were developed. The 1985 models took on pedestal-mounted bucket seats straight from the US-built Renault Alliance, in order to give more toe-room for rear passengers. From 1989, rear shoulder belts and an AM/FM stero radio were standard equipment, and that year also saw the arrival of a new overhead console, which was standard on Limited models and optional on the Laredo. A sunroof was optional for Sport models from 1992, and that year leather became optional for the Laredo. Then for 1994, all models were equipped with a third, high-mounted stoplamp and side door beams to meet new Federal requirements for this class of vehicle. The early 1990s also

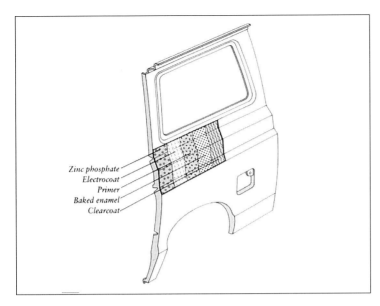

saw a driver's side airbag become standard equipment, with a passenger's airbag an extra-cost option.

Further revisions
The XJ range had been a massive success from the very beginning, and the millionth example was driven off the assembly lines at Toledo on March 22, 1990. It was a Cherokee Limited, with the four-door body found on 85% of all the XJ models built in the previous six and a half years. Yet more than 2 million XJ models had been sold worldwide by the time the next major changes were announced at the Detroit Auto Show in January 1997.

The new 1997 models had been redeveloped at a cost of $215 million, and at their heart was a monocoque stiffer by 43%, which improved torsional rigidity as well as making for greater ride comfort, better interior refinement and more precise handling. Their most obvious exterior changes were a new steel tailgate with a more curved profile, new tail-lights and a softer, more rounded frontal design. This featured a new seven-slot grille similar to that of the ZJ

Zinc phosphate
Electrocoat
Primer
Baked enamel
Clearcoat

Jeep were proud of their body protection measures. The steel panels were first galvanized, then subjected to a five-coat paint process.

The Cherokee was a massive success in the UK during the 1990s. This is a UK-market 4.0 Limited SE.

models, rounded wings, new sculpted bumpers, flared wheelarches and a new air dam.

Interior refinement had been improved with a package of measures designed to counter noise, vibration and harshness, while the interior design had also been given a major makeover. The restyled dashboard had lost the slab-fronted look of the earlier models and now had a much more rounded, softer appearance. It used a modular design of instrument panel which simplified the production of vehicles with both left- and right-hand drive in the same factory at Toledo. Needless to say, it incorporated dual airbags as standard equipment. The heating and ventilating system had also been thoroughly redesigned, with an increase in airflow of up to 30%. Other improvements included a new ABS system and – for the first time on models destined for Europe – a third brake light mounted high up at the rear. Chrysler also claimed that overall quality had been improved as well, as a result of major investment in new or reconditioned body press tools.

In this revitalized form, the XJ range is expected to continue into the 21st century, although it is unlikely that any more major changes will be made before it ceases production. The XJ has already earned its place in history as the model which really saved the Jeep marque; indeed, without it, Chrysler would probably never have bought Jeep in 1987. There is a certain irony about the fact that the initial development of this hugely successful vehicle was funded by Renault, who pulled out of their alliance with AMC just a little too soon to reap the full rewards of their investment.

The Comanche
Like the J-series models before it, the XJ range sired a utility model, which was announced in April 1985. However, the Comanche was no heavy-duty machine like the older Jeep trucks. Born into the age of the fashionable sporty mini-truck, it was a replacement for the Scrambler or CJ-8 (which went out of production in 1986). Like the rest of the XJ range, it was of unitary construction, and this fact certainly deterred some buyers who wanted a vehicle for heavy commercial work. However, Jeep had a different set

Despite excellent on-road behaviour for everyday use, the XJ never lost sight of Jeep's all-terrain roots.

Just below the top of the range in Britain in the mid-1990s was the Cherokee 4.0 Limited. Compare the wheels here with those on the SE model pictured on page 103.

The pick-up derivative of the XJ range was the Comanche. This is a 1989 Comanche SporTruck . . .

of buyers in mind, and with this model they really turned their back on the rural pick-up market in which they had done so well since the introduction of the original Jeep Truck in 1946.

Available initially with four-cylinder, V6 or Renault turbodiesel power, the Comanche came with either five-speed manual (built by Peugeot in France) or three-speed automatic transmission. From the beginning, 4x2 versions were also available, although 4x4 types were always more popular. For 1987, the V6 engine was dropped in favour of the new 4-litre in-line six, and the three-speed automatic was replaced by the Aisin-Warner four-speed overdrive type. During the 1989 model-year, new five-speed manual gearboxes were also introduced, made in this instance by Aisin Seiki.

The first Comanches came on a 119in wheelbase with a 7.5ft pick-up bed, but for 1987 this was joined by a 113in model with a 6ft bed. There were both 4x2 and 4x4

drivetrains from the beginning, and the Comanche came in base, X, and XLS trim levels, the latter easily distinguished by its chromed grille. However, for 1987 the marketing changed, to focus on a new performance model called the Eliminator, which had the new 4-litre engine in the lightest 4x2 short-bed structure. Graphics, low-profile tyres and 10-hole alloy wheels completed the picture. Meanwhile, other models were renamed as SporTruck and Pioneer. Eliminators were entered for the mini-pick-up class of the SCCA Race Truck Challenge, in which the Comanche was outright winner in 1987 and 1988.

However, the booming sales which accompanied this success collapsed for 1989. Chrysler Jeep attempted to restore the position with a 4x4 Eliminator option for 1990, and then with a new Sport package for 1992, but the public had lost interest. So Chrysler, understandably more interested in promoting its Dodge products in the mini-truck market, dropped the Comanche for 1993.

CHAPTER 9

The ZJ luxury cruiser

Grand Cherokee and Grand Wagoneer

Each of the Jeep brand's owners has made its mark on the company's products. When Kaiser took over in 1954, it greatly expanded the company's overseas operations, and when American Motors took over in 1970, it widened the appeal of Jeep vehicles. French money from the Renault concern which took an important shareholding in the company from 1979 allowed the company to invest in more modern vehicles during the 1980s. Chrysler's impact was felt in the 1992 Grand Cherokee, introduced in January that year at the Detroit Auto Show.

When Chrysler took over in 1987, plans for a new model to replace the XJ range in 1990 were already well advanced. The project was named ZJ, following on in logical sequence from the XJ itself and the YJ Wrangler. Initial ideas had been discussed in 1983, the project had been defined by September 1984, and by July 1986 everything seemed to be on target.

However, Chrysler had other ideas. Jeep's new owners saw no pressing need to replace the XJ range, which was selling strongly. On the other hand, they did see a need to compete in the luxury 4x4 class which had been opened up during 1987 by the first imports of the Range Rover. Mitsubishi were already pushing their Pajero (Shogun) models further upmarket into the luxury class, and Toyota were known to be working on a new super-Land Cruiser for 1989 introduction. Clearly, the luxury sport-utility market would soon be hotly contested, and Jeep could not afford to lose face by failing to put up a credible contender.

So the ZJ project was halted at the end of 1987, and

Chrysler redefined its aim. The new Jeep would now be a luxury-market sport-utility model to be sold alongside the XJ. It would be a sporty, stylish and luxurious vehicle with all the off-road ability traditional to the marque. In order to avoid any compromises in the design, it would be designed without a utility derivative. And above all, its manufacturing costs would have to be low so that showroom prices would also be low and the vehicle would offer first-rate value for money as one of its principal attractions.

Low manufacturing costs could only be achieved through investment in the very latest manufacturing technology, and it was also clear that the ZJ could not be squeezed into the space vacated by the old Grand Wagoneers when they ceased production at Toledo. So Chrysler determined to build a brand-new assembly plant for the ZJ. These decisions, of course, delayed the project, although a lot of the work originally done was retained when work started again in 1988. The Jeep design engineers were now working towards an early 1992 launch, which also gave Chrysler time to build the new Jefferson North assembly plant in Detroit.

By the end of 1988, the ZJ design team had settled on a styling concept which closely anticipated the eventual production model. Under the name of Concept I, this was revealed as a full-size mock-up at the Detroit Auto Show in January 1989, thus stealing a march on Toyota, whose new 80-series Land Cruiser would not be announced until later in the year. The new Jeep was not yet ready for production, and no-one would officially confirm that the Concept I

mock-up was a foretaste of the production vehicle to come. Nevertheless, few industry insiders doubted that this was the forthcoming Grand Wagoneer replacement, and none of them could fail to be impressed by its striking new styling.

Body styling and construction
While the new Jeep still looked like a credible off-road vehicle, its station wagon styling was even more car-like than that of the Cherokee and – more important still – it looked very much more streamlined, with a sloping bonnet line. It was quite clear from the low height of Concept I that the Jeep engineers were once again working on a unitary body for the new model, and the overall dimensions made clear that this would be even bigger than the unitary body on the XJ Cherokee. What Jeep were planning, and went on to execute, was the largest unitary-construction 4x4 yet seen.

This was no mean engineering feat, particularly as costs had to be kept down. Yet the Jeep engineers managed to make the unitary bodyshell so much stiffer than that of the

XJ Cherokee that it was possible to fit a sunroof without losing body rigidity to an unacceptable degree. Moreover, the low-slung design of the ZJ body overcame the XJ's other main failing of poor headroom without compromising underbody clearance for off-road work. The spare wheel was kept high up out of the way (although its position inside the load bay did eat into the load space), and the single-piece, lift-up tailgate, like that of a conventional estate car, came with a sensible roller luggage blind which lifted up with it.

Mechanical elements and equipment
As far as the suspension was concerned, there was no doubt that coil springs were the way to go. The XJ Cherokee already had coil springs at the front, as did the Mitsubishi Pajero; and the class-leading Range Rover had the all-round coil springs which were expected to feature on the upcoming Land Cruiser. Coil-spring suspension had two important advantages, the first being that it permitted a softer ride on the road and the second that it allowed much

greater axle articulation for off-road work than conventional leaf springs. So the Jeep engineers specified all-round coil-spring suspension for the ZJ model, allied to the gas dampers which were giving such good results on the XJ Cherokee. They gave this new suspension the name of Quadra-Coil.

At the rear, a four-link axle location system was designed to improve the on-road handling, and – in typical Jeep fashion – this was given its own name of Quadra-Link when production began. Meanwhile, at the front the Jeep designers decided to stay with a live axle rather than go for the independent suspension favoured by the Mitsubishi Pajero. Both the Range Rover and the Land Cruiser did likewise, for the very good reason that the independent suspension proved detrimental to off-road ability even though it offered on-road handling benefits.

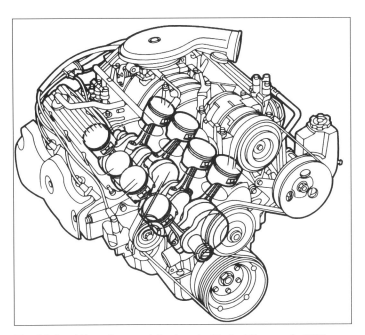

The 5.2-litre V8 engine was introduced with the ZJ range in 1992.

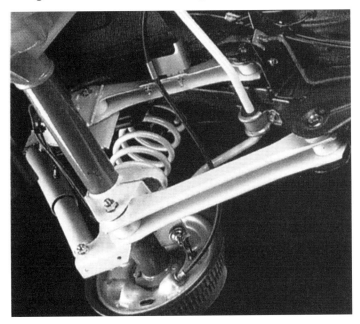

The ZJ models were the first Jeeps to feature all-round coil-spring suspension, known as Quadra-Coil.

Steering and braking also received careful attention. Once again, a recirculating-ball steering system was employed, with speed-sensitive power assistance on top models. This proved to be something of a disappointment because it was over-light and lacked feel. Braking, however, was much more successful. It featured ventilated discs on the front wheels, with drums at the rear and both power assistance and ABS as standard equipment. Solid rear disc brakes were optional, but standard for some markets.

As for transmissions, there was no question that top models should have Quadra-Trac permanent four-wheel drive with a dual-ratio transfer box and the latest four-speed overdrive automatic gearbox. Lesser models would have to make do with manual gearboxes and the Command-Trac or Selec-Trac transmissions, and in due course the traditional 4x2 versions would also put in an appearance. A viscous-

An early example of the Grand Cherokee Limited with the optional 5.2-litre V8 engine; this one was exported to Britain.

coupled central differential was also specified for all 4x4 models, so that they could be used in four-wheel-drive mode on paved surfaces, and a limited-slip Powr-Loc differential in the rear axle was made standard equipment. Safety regulations in the USA demanded an interlock mechanism on manuals, which prevented the engine from being started unless the clutch was disengaged.

The existing 4-litre six-cylinder could be used as the entry-level engine, but something more powerful was needed for top models. So Chrysler decided to use the 318ci (5.2-litre) V8 engine developed for its Dodge Durango sport-utility range. This promised 215bhp and a massive 285lb.ft of torque, developed at a high enough crankshaft speed to give real punch for overtaking manoeuvres.

Since the XJ range had been developed, the luxury sport-utility market had become much more demanding, so the customer expectations which Chrysler were planning to meet with the ZJ range were different in many ways from those which had helped to shape the XJ. High levels of

equipment were important now, so the ZJ range was developed with the expectation that air conditioning, cruise control, heated front seats with power adjustment, and heated door mirrors would all be needed on the majority of models sold. The air conditioning was a new system, with automatic climate control. It went without saying that there would be tilt steering and central locking as standard, and in order to meet forthcoming safety regulations, the new model also had to be equipped with airbags. The first Grand Cherokees had only the driver's side bag as standard, but later examples came with both driver and front passenger airbags.

The European dimension
Another of Chrysler's key market goals also had a major impact on the ZJ, and this was expansion into Europe. It was already clear that the XJ Cherokee had some quite serious shortcomings as far as European buyers were concerned, perhaps the most glaring being its uncompromisingly American dashboard configuration. The

new ZJ was intended to compete for sales against luxury cars as well as luxury sport-utility models, so the designers took a long look at the best dashboard designs from European luxury car manufacturers. As a result, the ZJ ended up with an exemplary dashboard and ash veneer trim, which not only appealed to European buyers but also fitted the vogue for European luxury cars in the USA itself. It was both attractive to look at and ergonomically sound, and in this it actually outdid some of its competitors – especially the Range Rover of 1992 vintage. Among its advanced features was a unique-fit cassette-radio and CD player control centre, intended to discourage theft.

From the beginning, Chrysler had intended that the new ZJ range should offer exceptional value for money in what was already a hotly-contested market. Quite clearly, if vehicles had to be shipped from the Toledo assembly plant to Europe, their showroom prices would be inflated by an unacceptable amount. So a plan was drawn up for the ZJ to be built in Europe as well as in the USA, so that it could be sold with the same price advantage against competitive vehicles as it was to enjoy in the USA.

Chrysler was already establishing a manufacturing base in the Austrian town of Graz, where the old-established Steyr company would begin to assemble the Plymouth Voyager for European consumption in the early 1990s. So it was here that overseas manufacture of the ZJ would be undertaken – and, as it turned out, not only for Europe. To simplify the production lines in Detroit, manufacture of all right-hand-drive ZJs was centralised at Graz. Thus the Austrian factory would build vehicles not only for Britain, but also for the other right-hand-drive markets of Australia, Japan, the Middle East, New Zealand and South Africa. Production of the ZJ started at Graz in October 1994 on assembly lines with a capacity of 40,000 vehicles a year. The standard engine for all markets would be the 4-litre six-cylinder, with 174bhp.

There was another important dimension to Chrysler's drive for Jeep sales in Europe. This was that a diesel engine option was essential for successful sales of a sport-utility – even one aimed at the luxury class – whereas such an option was almost never offered in the USA. For the Voyager,

Off-road ability of the latest model was every bit as good as the Jeep tradition demanded.

Chrysler had already struck a deal with the Italian diesel engine specialists VM to buy their 2.5-litre four-cylinder turbocharged diesel engine. This was an indirect-injection unit which could trace its ancestry back to the late 1970s and already had a good track record in sport-utility vehicles. It had been optional in the Range Rover since 1989, and in later years would also be used in the Vauxhall/Opel Frontera as well as Jeep's own XJ Cherokee. So the Italian engine, known as an HR 494, was added to the ZJ programme. It became available in January 1997.

Before right-hand-drive production started in 1994, a few American-built left-hand-drive models were exported to

This 1996 Grand Cherokee 4.0 Limited is one of the Graz-built models, and here shows off the distinctive wheels of the time.

some European countries. Small numbers were put on sale in Britain, where the only model available had the 5.2-litre V8 engine. These 'preview' models were snapped up for their exclusivity value, and feedback from the buyers allowed Chrysler Jeep to fine-tune the European-built model to suit local tastes. Most notable among the changes which were made to the American-built vehicle were in the suspension settings, which were made firmer to suit European buyers.

Trim packages

The Grand Cherokee went on sale in April 1992 after being previewed at the Detroit Auto Show in January. There were three trim levels – base, Laredo and Limited – and all models had the 4-litre engine. However, the autumn brought a fourth model at the top of the range, which took on the name of the old Grand Wagoneer and came with the 5.2-litre V8 and automatic transmission as standard. At the same time, the V8 engine became optional on all versions of the Grand Cherokee.

Laredo models had a chromed grille, while the Limited grille was painted in the body colour; the Laredo wheels were also chunky-looking five-spoke alloys, which contrasted with the multi-spoked Limited type (later replaced by a style with more intricate shaping and a polished finish). Laredo upholstery was cloth, while the Limited models had leather. Limited models also had generally higher levels of equipment, and most visibly had front foglamps set into the spoiler. It was Chrysler's proud boast that the only options on the Limited model were a CD player and a sunroof; and later, even these would become part of the standard equipment. Grand Wagoneer models came with the multi-spoke alloy wheels as standard, and a swathe of fake wood trim along each side of their bodies. Leather upholstery was standard, of course, and the equipment specification was as complete as any luxury-market buyer could wish for.

The ZJ range was an immediate and massive sales success, but Chrysler did not rest on its laurels. For 1993, it introduced 4x2 models with base and Laredo trim levels,

A 1997 UK-specification Grand Cherokee Laredo. Note the chunky spoked alloy wheels, chromed grille, absence of foglamps in the front spoiler, and the 'Laredo' name on the flank protection panels under the 'Grand Cherokee' badge.

The cheaper models had cloth upholstery, as seen here on a right-hand-drive Grand Cherokee Laredo.

and then 1994 saw the base models redesignated SE, while the Grand Wagoneer was discontinued, leaving the Limited at the top of the tree. Side door beams were also standardized across the range that year.

Statistics give a good impression of the ZJ's success. During 1994, this one range of models accounted for half of all Jeeps sold worldwide, and by the middle of 1995 – three and a half years after its launch – it had already sold an astonishing 650,000 copies. By the end of 1997, when it had been on sale for six years, it had racked up sales of over 1,605,000. Inevitably, this success had made the manufacturers of competitive sport-utility vehicles sit up and take notice, and since the Grand Cherokee's launch they had introduced new models and upgraded older ones in order to remain competitive. Perhaps the biggest threat came from the second-generation Range Rover, introduced in the autumn of 1994 and featuring exceptionally high equipment levels and a 4.6-litre V8 engine, which endowed top models with a 125mph maximum speed. Keen marketing of the Range Rover, especially in the USA, also

The 1998 Grand Cherokee 5.9 Limited LX shows off the latest ZJ range features: Ultra-Star alloy wheels, restyled sill panels, a mesh grille and a redesigned roof rack.

gave it a snob appeal which the Grand Cherokee was unable to emulate. Then in 1998 came the new 100-series Toyota Land Cruiser, with its 4.7-litre V8 petrol engine.

Rising to the challenge
So Chrysler Jeep made sure that the Grand Cherokee was able to take on these challenges. The performance issue was tackled with the introduction at the very end of 1997 of a new Grand Cherokee 5.9 Limited LX, with a claimed 125mph top speed. This had a 5.9-litre V8 engine with 237bhp and a huge 348lb.ft of torque, once again borrowed from the Dodge sport-utility range. It was manufactured only with left-hand drive, even in Graz (nevertheless, 100 or so examples were brought to Britain for sale through Jeep dealers, much as had happened with the 5.2-litre Grand Cherokee before right-hand-drive production had begun). The model was distinguished by special badging, and more obviously by new Ultra-Star star-pattern sparkle-silver alloy

wheels. There were also unique sill panels, a honeycomb mesh behind the painted grille, air intake slats on the hood panel, and a new style of adjustable roof rack.

As far as the snob-appeal issue was concerned, a link-up with Orvis, the USA's leading supplier of fly-fishing equipment, was intended to do the trick. The Jeep Grand Cherokee Orvis was introduced at the beginning of 1998, and added new features to the equipment of the Limited model. Most of these came from the 5.9 Limited LX, which donated its Ultra-Star wheels, mesh grille, new sills and roof rails, and bonnet louvres. In Britain, the Austrian-built version of the Orvis came in just three colours – Forest Green, Bright Platinum Pearlcoat and Deep Slate Pearlcoat, the latter two being unique to the model.

Thus, by 1998, the Grand Cherokee remained the top Jeep model, and its makers were intent on keeping it at the top of the luxury 4x4 market. Although other competitors had emulated its high equipment levels, no others had yet

While quite clearly related to the original ZJ range, the much-revised 1999 Grand Cherokee was intended to offer even more luxury.

successfully matched it on value for money, and none had matched its sleek, low-slung styling.

A LOOK INTO THE FUTURE

The second-generation Grand Cherokee

In June 1998, Chrysler Jeep announced that the ZJ Grand Cherokee models would be replaced in the US market that autumn by a brand-new Grand Cherokee. European models, built once again at Graz in Austria, were expected to follow in early 1999.

Riding on the same 2,691mm (105.9in) wheelbase as the old model, the new Grand Cherokee was 112mm longer, 64.5mm wider and 40mm taller, with a track 38mm wider. Step-in height was reduced by 28mm for easy entry, yet the seating position was 25mm higher to give an enhanced 'command-of-the-road' feel. Publicity material claimed that the interior would be more luxurious than ever.

The petrol engines in the new model were to be the 4.0-litre six-cylinder in 193bhp form and a new 4.7-litre V8 promising 227bhp at 4,600rpm and 294lb-ft of torque at 3,200rpm. In addition, there was to be an all-new OHV five-cylinder direct-injection intercooled turbodiesel, with 148bhp at 4,000rpm and 275lb-ft of torque at 2,000rpm. This had been developed by Jeep in conjunction with Detroit Diesel and VM, and all models were to have four-speed overdrive automatic transmissions and Quadra-Trac II on-demand four-wheel-drive systems, using an N247 two-speed transfer case. Once again, there was to be a live axle at each end.

Concepts and promises

The 1990s have also seen a number of Jeep concept vehicles displayed at Motor Shows, and these have offered some insight into the thinking behind future Jeep products – although they do not necessarily reflect any specific future vehicle.

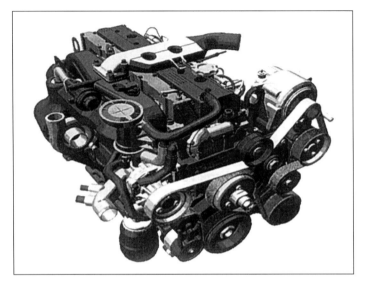

After the five-cylinder diesel, a new four-cylinder four-valve type is expected.

The Ecco concept vehicle appeared on the show circuit in 1993 and was described as an ideas vehicle for a future Wrangler-type model. Designed by Trevor Creed, it had a 100.3in wheelbase and a three-cylinder, two-stroke engine. Although the side panels were fixed, it had a folding fabric roof.

Nearer reality, perhaps, was the Icon concept vehicle, again supposedly revealing thoughts on a future Wrangler-type model.

This Jeepster concept car started life as a theoretical crossover-model project, and appeared at the Detroit Auto Show in January 1998. It coupled the power and excitement of a sports car with the go-anywhere ability traditional to Jeep. Under the hood was a 32-valve version of the 4.7-litre V8 engine planned for the new Grand Cherokee, and the vehicle had electronically height-adjustable suspension with a range of 4in to give optimum aerodynamics for road use or high ground clearance for off-road use.

In addition, Chrysler's Francois J Castaing, now Executive Vice President International and General Manager, Power Train Operations, has promised a new 2.5-litre turbodiesel for introduction in 2001. This will have twin overhead camshafts with four valves per cylinder, and a high-pressure common-rail direct-injection fuel system. Some 136bhp are expected, with fuel consumption around 15% lower than in the current VM 2.5-litre turbodiesel.

APPENDIX A

Technical specifications

Notes: 1. These specifications are arranged **in chronological order of the models' introduction**. Related models (*eg* CJ-5A and DJ-5A) are grouped together under the introduction date of the earlier model.
2. All dates refer to model-year only.

Jeep MB/Ford GPW (1941-1945)
Engine: 134.2ci (2,199cc) Go-Devil side-valve four-cylinder with 3.125in (79.4mm) bore and 4.375in (111.1mm) stroke, 6.48:1 compression ratio, single-barrel carburettor, 60bhp at 3,600rpm and 105lb.ft at 2,000rpm.
Transmission: Three-speed primary gearbox with synchromesh on second and third gears; ratios 2.67:1, 1.56:1, 1.00:1. Two-speed transfer gearbox with selectable four-wheel drive.
Steering, suspension and brakes: Cam-and-lever steering. Semi-elliptic leaf springs all round with hydraulic dampers. Drum brakes.
Dimensions: Wheelbase 80in (2,030mm). Front and rear track 48.25in (1,225mm). Length 122in (3,350mm). Width 62in (1,600mm). Height 69in (1,750mm) with top raised. Kerb weight (typical) 2,453lb (1,113kg).

CJ-2A (1945-1949)
As for MB, except as follows:
Dimensions: Length 123.12in (3,127mm). Width 57.12in (1,451mm). Height 64in (1,626mm). Kerb weight (typical) 2,240lb (1,016kg).

Station Wagon (1946-1955)
Utility Wagon (1956-1965)
Panel Delivery (1947-1951)
Sedan Delivery (1952-1962)
Engines: 134ci (2,199cc) Go-Devil side-valve four-cylinder with 3.125in (79.34mm) bore and 4.375in (111.1mm) stroke, 6.48:1 compression ratio, single-barrel carburettor, 63bhp at 4,000rpm and 105lb.ft at 2,000rpm; standard from 1948-50.

134ci (2,199cc) Hurricane overhead inlet and side exhaust valve four-cylinder with 3.125in (79.34mm) bore and 4.375in (111.1mm) stroke, 6.9:1 compression ratio (1950-52) or 7.4:1 compression ratio (1953-63), single-barrel carburettor, 72bhp at 4,000rpm (75bhp from 1953) and 114lb.ft at 2,000rpm; standard from 1950-63.

148.5ci (2,433cc) Lightning side-valve six-cylinder with 3.0in (76.2mm) bore and 3.50in (88.9mm) stroke, 6.42:1 compression ratio, single-barrel carburettor, 72bhp at 4,000rpm and 117lb.ft at 1,600rpm; optional 1948-50.

161ci (2,638cc) Lightning side-valve six-cylinder with 3.125in (79.37mm) bore and 3.50in (88.9mm) stroke, 7.4:1 compression ratio, single-barrel carburettor, 75bhp at 4,000rpm and 117lb.ft at 1,600rpm; optional 1950-54.

226ci (3,703cc) Super Hurricane overhead inlet and side exhaust valve six-cylinder with 3.31in (84mm) bore and 4.38in (111.25mm) stroke, 7.3:1 compression ratio, single-barrel carburettor, 115bhp at 3,650rpm (105bhp from 1959) and 190lb.ft at 1,800rpm; optional from 1954-62.

230ci (3,769cc) Tornado OHC six-cylinder with 3.34in (84.8mm) bore and 4.38in (111.25mm) stroke, 8.5:1 compression ratio, single-barrel carburettor, 140bhp at 4,000rpm and 210lb.ft at 1,750rpm; optional 1962-63.
Transmission: Single-dry-plate clutch. Three-speed primary gearbox; overdrive optional (1946 and 1956-65) or standard (1947-55). Gear ratios 2.60:1, 1.63:1, 1.00:1, overdrive 0.70:1. Rear-wheel drive only; selectable four-wheel drive optional from 1949. Two-speed transfer gearbox on 4x4 models. Axle ratio 4.88:1; 5.38:1 optional.
Steering, suspension and brakes: Cam-and-lever steering; optional power assistance from 1958. 4x2 models (1946-53) have independent 'Planadyne' front suspension with control arms and single transverse leaf spring; later 4x2 models have beam front axle with semi-elliptic leaf springs. All 4x4 models have live axles front and rear, with semi-elliptic leaf springs. All-drum brakes.
Dimensions: Wheelbase 104in (2,642mm). Front track 55.25in

(1,403mm), 4x2 models or 57in (1,448mm), 4x4 models. Rear track 57in (1,448mm). Length 176.25in (4,477mm). Width 71.8in (1,824mm). Height 71in (1,803mm). Kerb weight (typical) 2,898lb (1314kg).

Jeep Truck (1947-1963)
As for Station Wagon, except as follows:
Engines: 134ci Go-Devil four-cylinder standard 1947-50; 134ci Hurricane four-cylinder standard 1950-63; 226ci Super Hurricane six-cylinder optional 1954-63.
Transmission: Selectable four-wheel drive optional from 1947 and standard from 1953; rear-wheel drive only standard from 1947 and to special order only from 1953.
Suspension: All two-wheel-drive models with front beam axle and semi-elliptic springs.
Dimensions: Wheelbase 118in (2,997mm). Length 175in (4,445mm). Kerb weight (typical) 2,468lb (1,119kg).

CJ-3A (1948-1953)
DJ-3A (1955-1965)
As for CJ-2A, except as follows:
Transmission: DJ-3A with rear-wheel drive only.
Dimensions: Length 123in (3,124mm). Height 66.37in (1,686mm).

Jeepster (1948-1950)
As for Station Wagon, except as follows:
Engines: 134ci Go-Devil four-cylinder standard 1948-49; 134ci Hurricane four-cylinder standard 1950; 148.5ci Lightning six-cylinder optional 1949; 161ci Lighting six-cylinder optional 1950.
Transmission: Overdrive standard 1948-49 and optional 1950. Rear-wheel drive only.
Suspension and brakes: 'Planadyne' independent front suspension on all models. 300 1950 models (sold as '1951' models) fitted with larger 'mountain' brakes.
Dimensions: Length 174in (4,420mm). Height 62in (1,575mm). Width 69in (1,753mm). Kerb weight (typical) 2,890lb (1,311kg).

CJ-3B (1952-1968)
As for CJ-3A, except as follows:
Engine: 134ci (2,199cc) Hurricane overhead inlet and side exhaust valve four-cylinder with 3.125in (79.34mm) bore and 4.375in (111.1mm) stroke, 7.4:1 compression ratio, single-barrel carburettor, 75bhp at 4,000rpm and 114lb.ft at 2,000rpm.
Dimensions: Length 129.88in (3,299mm). Width 68.88in (1,749mm). Height 67.75in (1,721mm). Kerb weight (typical) 2,243lb (1,017kg).

CJ-5 (1955-1983)
CJ-5A (1964-1967)
DJ-5A (1964-1973)
Engines: 134ci (2,199cc) Hurricane overhead inlet and side exhaust valve four-cylinder with 3.125in (79.34mm) bore and 4.375in (111.1mm) stroke, 7.4:1 compression ratio, single-barrel carburettor, 75bhp at 4,000rpm and 114 lb.ft at 2,000rpm; standard 1955-71 and fitted to all DJ-5A models.

192ci (3,146cc) Perkins 4.192 four-cylinder indirect-injection diesel with 3.5in (88.9mm) bore and 5in (127mm) stroke, 62bhp at 3,000rpm and 143lb.ft at 1,350rpm; optional for export from 1965.

225ci (3,687cc) Dauntless OHV V6 with 3.75in (95.25mm) bore and 3.4in (86.36mm) stroke, 9.0:1 compression ratio, two-barrel carburettor, 160bhp at 4,200rpm and 235lb.ft at 2,400rpm; optional 1965-71.

232ci (3,801cc) OHV six-cylinder with 3.75in (95.25mm) bore and 3.5in (88.9mm) stroke, 8.0:1 compression ratio, single-barrel carburettor, 100bhp at 3,600rpm and 185lb.ft at 1,800rpm; standard 1972-78.

258ci (4,228cc) OHV six-cylinder with 3.75in (95.25mm) bore and 3.9in (99.06mm) stroke, 8.0:1 compression ratio, single-barrel carburettor (1972-78) or two-barrel carburettor (1979-83), 110bhp at 3,500rpm and 195lb.ft at 2,000rpm (1972-78) or 114bhp at 3,200rpm and 210lb.ft at 2,000rpm (1979-83); optional 1972-83.

304ci (4,982cc) OHV V8 with 3.75in (95.25mm) bore and 3.44in (87.38mm) stroke, 8.4:1 compression ratio, four-barrel (1972-78) or two-barrel (1979-81) carburettor, 150bhp at 4,200rpm and 245lb.ft at 2,500rpm (1972-78) or 130bhp at 3,200rpm and 225lb.ft at 2,200rpm (1979-81); optional 1972-81.

151ci (2,474cc) Hurricane (Pontiac Iron Duke) OHV four-cylinder with 4.00in (101.6mm) bore and 3.00in (76.2mm) stroke, 8.2:1 compression ratio, two-barrel carburettor, 86bhp at 4,000rpm and 125lb.ft at 2,600rpm; standard 1980-83.
Transmission: Three-speed primary gearbox with synchromesh on second and third gears; ratios 2.67:1, 1.56:1, 1.00:1 (standard 1955-67); overdrive optional from 1961. Three-speed all-synchromesh gearbox (standard 1968-79). Four-speed all-synchromesh gearbox (standard 1980-83). Four-speed gearbox with synchromesh on second, third and fourth gears; ratios 4.02:1, 2.41:1, 1.41:1, 1.00:1 (optional 1960-76). Four-speed gearbox with synchromesh on second, third and fourth gears; ratios 6.32:1, 3.00:1, 1.69:1, 1.00:1 (optional 1977-83). Two-speed transfer gearbox with selectable four-wheel drive on all CJ-5 models; low ratio 2.45:1 (1955-71), 2.03:1 (1972-79), 2.62:1 (1980-83); DJ-5A models with rear-wheel drive only. Axle ratio 5.38:1 standard (1955-64); 4.27:1 optional (1960-64); 4.27:1 standard and 5.38:1 optional (1965-71, four-cylinder models); 3.92:1 standard

(V6 models); 4.88:1 (V6 models with overdrive); 3.73:1 standard and 4.27:1 optional (1972); 3.54:1 standard and 4.09:1 optional (1980, four-cylinder models); 3.07:1 standard and 3.54:1 optional (1980, six-cylinder and V8 models); 2.73:1 standard (1981-83, all models).

Steering, suspension and brakes: Cam-and-lever steering. Semi-elliptic leaf springs all round with hydraulic dampers. Drum brakes; front disc brakes with power assistance optional from 1977.

Dimensions: Wheelbase 81in (2,057mm), 1955-71; 84in (2,134mm) 1972-76; 83.5in (2,121mm) 1977-1983. Front track 48.5in (1,232mm) 1955-71; 51.5in (1,308mm) 1972-83. Rear track 48.5in (1,232mm), 1955-71; 50in (1,270mm) 1972-83. Length 135.6in (3,444mm) 1955-71; 138.9in (3,528mm), 1972-83. Width 68.6in (1,742mm). Height 67in (1,702mm). Kerb weight (typical) 2,274lb (1,031kg), four-cylinder and V6; 2,420lb (1,098kg), in-line six-cylinder; 2,440lb (1,107kg), V8.

CJ-6 (1955-1981)
CJ-6A (1964-1967)
As for contemporary CJ-5, except as follows:
Dimensions: Wheelbase 101in (2,565mm) 1955-71; 104in (2,642mm) 1972-76; 103.5in (2,629mm) 1977-81. Length 155.56in (3,951mm) 1955-71; 147.9in (3,757mm) 1972-81. Kerb weight (typical) 2,413lb (1,094kg).

FC-150 Forward Control (1957-1964)
As for contemporary CJ-5, except as follows:
Engine: 134ci (2,199cc) Hurricane four-cylinder engine optionally available with 7.4:1 compression for high altitudes.
Dimensions: Length 147.5in (3,746mm). Width 71.375in (1,813mm). Height 77.375in (1,965mm).

FC-170 Forward Control (1957-1964)
As for contemporary CJ-6, except as follows:
Engine: 226ci (3,703cc) Super Hurricane overhead inlet and side exhaust valve six-cylinder with four-bearing crankshaft, 3.31in (84mm) bore and 4.38in (111.25mm) stroke, 6.86:1 compression ratio (7.3:1 optional for high altitudes), single-barrel carburettor, 105bhp at 3,600rpm and 190lb.ft at 1,400rpm.
Transmission: Axle ratio 4.88:1.
Dimensions: Wheelbase 103.5in (2,629mm). Length 180.5in (4,584mm). Width 76.5in (1,943mm). Height 79.375in (2,016mm).

FJ-3A Fleetvan (1961-1964)
As for contemporary CJ-5, except as follows:
Dimensions: Length, width, height and kerb weight details not available.

Wagoneer (1963-1991)
Engine: 230ci (3,770cc) Tornado OHC six-cylinder, with 3.34in (85mm) bore and 4.38in (111mm) stroke, 8.5:1 compression ratio (7.5:1 optional, 1965), 140bhp at 4,000rpm (133bhp at 4,000rpm with low compression) and 210lb.ft at 1,750rpm; all models 1963-65.

232ci (3,802cc) Hi-Torque Six OHV six-cylinder with 3.75in (95.25mm) bore and 3.5in (88.9mm) stroke, 8.0:1 compression ratio, single-barrel carburettor, 145bhp at 4,300rpm and 215lb.ft at 1,600rpm; standard 1966-72.

258ci (4,228cc) OHV six-cylinder with 3.75in (95.25mm) bore and 3.9in (99.06mm) stroke, 8.0:1 compression ratio, single-barrel carburettor, 110bhp at 3,500rpm and 195lb.ft at 2,000rpm (1972-78); two-barrel carburettor and 114bhp (1979); 8.3:1 compression ratio, two-barrel carburettor, 118bhp at 3,200rpm and 205lb.ft at 1,800rpm (1980); 110bhp (1981-86); standard 1972-86.

304ci (4,982cc) OHV V8 with 3.75in (95.25mm) bore and 3.44in (87.38mm) stroke, 8.4:1 compression ratio, two-barrel carburettor, 150bhp at 4,200rpm and 245lb.ft at 2,500rpm; optional 1972-78.

327ci (5,360cc) Vigilante OHV V8 with 4in (101.6mm) bore and 3.25in (82.55mm) stroke, 8.7:1 compression ratio, two-barrel carburettor (four-barrel in Super Wagoneer 1966-68), 250bhp at 4,700rpm (270bhp in Super Wagoneer) and 340lb.ft at 2,600rpm; optional 1965-68.

350ci (5,730cc) Dauntless OHV V8 with 3.80in (96.5mm) bore and 3.85in (97.8mm) stroke, 9.0:1 compression ratio, two-barrel carburettor, 230bhp at 4,400rpm and 350lb.ft at 2,400rpm; optional 1968-71.

360ci (5,899cc) V8 with 4.08in (103.6mm) bore and 3.44in (87.37mm) stroke, 8.5:1 compression ratio, two-barrel carburettor, 175bhp at 4,000rpm and 285lb.ft at 2,400rpm (optional 1972-86, standard 1987-91); four-barrel carburettor optional 1973-78 with 195bhp at 4,400rpm and 295lb.ft at 2,900rpm; 8.25:1 compression ratio from 1974; 1979 models with 8.25:1 compression ratio and two-barrel carburettor, 129bhp at 3,700rpm and 245lb.ft at 1,600rpm; 1980-86 models with 8.25:1 compression ratio and two-barrel carburettor, 160bhp at 3,400rpm and 280lb.ft at 1,500rpm; 1987-91 models with two-barrel carburettor, 144bhp and 280lb.ft at 1,500rpm.

401ci (6,571cc) OHV V8 with 4.165in (105.79mm) bore and 3.68in (93.47mm) stroke, 8.35:1 compression ratio and four-barrel carburettor, 215bhp at 4,400rpm and 320lb.ft at 2,800rpm (optional 1974-79).
Transmission: (1963-65) Three-speed manual primary gearbox standard; 4x2 models with all-synchromesh Warner T-86 (ratios 2.57:1, 1.55:1, 1.00:1) and 4x4 models with Warner T-90 (ratios

2.80:1, 1.55:1, 1.00:1) with synchromesh on second and third only. Overdrive option on 4x2 models. Three-speed GM Turbo-Hydramatic automatic optional (ratios 2.40:1, 1.47:1, 1.00:1). Dana Model 20 two-speed transfer box with 2.03:1 low ratio on 4x4 models. Axle ratio 4.09:1; 4.27:1 with overdrive and 3.73:1 with automatic.

(1966-72) As for 1963-65 models, but all models have 4x4 transmissions. Warner T-90 three-speed primary gearbox standard; optional Turbo-Hydramatic three-speed automatic; optional four-speed heavy-duty primary gearbox (ratios 6.32:1, 3.09:1, 1.68:1, 1.00:1).

(1973-79) All models with 4x4 transmissions. All-synchromesh three-speed primary gearbox standard (ratios 3.00:1, 1.83:1, 1.00:1); heavy-duty four-speed optional; Turbo-Hydramatic automatic optional (ratios 2.48:1, 1.48:1, 1.00:1). Two-speed transfer gearbox with selectable four-wheel drive on all 1973 manual models; Borg-Warner Quadra-Trac transfer gearbox with permanent four-wheel drive and optional low-ratio gearbox standard with automatic transmission from 1973 and standard on all models from 1974. Axle ratios 3.07:1 (with 360ci engine), 3.31:1 (1973 with Quadra-Trac), 3.54:1 (with 258ci and 401ci engines and optional with 360ci engines), 4.09:1 (optional with 258 engine).

(From 1980) All models with 4x4 transmissions. Tremec T-176 all-synchromesh four-speed primary gearbox (ratios 3.52:1, 2.27:1, 1.46:1, 1.00:1) standard on 1980 and 1981 models; Warner T5 five-speed primary gearbox standard from 1982; optional Torque-Flite three-speed automatic (with lock-up torque converter from 1981). Chrysler New Process 208 (Selec-Trac) two-speed transfer gearbox with 2.61:1 low ratio on manual models; Borg-Warner Quadra-Trac permanent four-wheel drive with viscous unit in centre differential and optional low-ratio gearbox on automatics. Axle ratio 3.31:1 on all models. Axle ratio 2.73:1.

Steering, suspension and brakes: Recirculating-ball steering with power assistance (optional 1963-73, standard 1974-91). All 4x4 models with semi-elliptic leaf springs all round; swing-axle independent front suspension with torsion bar springs standard on 4x2 models and optional on 4x4 models 1963-65. Front anti-roll bar optional 1976-91. Drum brakes all round; discs on the front wheels from 1967. Power-assisted brakes optional from 1967 and standard with disc front brakes.
Dimensions: Wheelbase 110in (2,794mm) 1963-73; 108.7in (2,761mm) from 1974. Front track 57.3in (1,455mm). Rear track 57.5in (1,460mm). Length 186.4in (4,734mm). Width 74.8in (1,900mm). Height 66.4in (1,686mm). Kerb weight (typical) 4,750lb (2,155kg).

Gladiator (1963-1969)
J-series (1970-1988)
As for contemporary Wagoneer, except as follows:
Engine: 230ci Tornado six-cylinder (1963-65); 232ci six-cylinder (1966-71); 350ci V8 (optional 1966-75); 258ci six-cylinder (standard 1972-88); 360ci V8 (optional 1972-88); 401ci V8 (optional 1976-80).
Dimensions: Wheelbase 120in (3,048mm) or 126in (3,200mm), 1963-69; 120in (3,048mm) or 132in (3,353mm) 1970-73; 118.7in (3,015mm) or 130.7in (3,320mm), 1974-78. Length 193.6in (4,917mm) with 118.7in wheelbase; 206in (5,232mm) with 130.7in wheelbase. Width 78.9in (2,004mm). Height 69in (1,753mm). Kerb weight (typical) 4,200lb (1,905kg).

Jeepster Convertible and Jeepster Commando (1967-1972)
Engine: 134ci (2,199cc) Hurricane overhead inlet and side exhaust valve four-cylinder with 3.125in (79.34mm) bore and 4.375in (111.1mm) stroke, 7.4:1 compression ratio, single-barrel carburettor, 75bhp at 4,000rpm and 114lb.ft at 2,000rpm; standard.

225ci (3,687cc) Dauntless OHV V6 with 3.75in (95.25mm) bore and 3.4in (86.36mm) stroke, 9.0:1 compression ratio, two-barrel carburettor, 160bhp at 4,200rpm and 235lb.ft at 2,400rpm; optional.
Transmission: Single-dry-plate clutch. Three-speed manual primary gearbox standard; four-speed manual and three-speed automatic optional. Gear ratios (automatic) 2.48:1, 1.48:1, 1.00:1 Two-speed transfer gearbox with 2.03:1 low ratio. Axle ratio 3.73:1.
Steering, suspension and brakes: Recirculating-ball steering with optional power assistance. Live axles with semi-elliptic leaf springs and Panhard rod on front axle. All-drum brakes with dual hydraulic circuit and power assistance standard.
Dimensions: Wheelbase 101in (2,565mm). Front and rear track 50in (1,270mm). Length 168.4in (4,277mm). Width 65.2in (1,656mm). Height 62.4in (1,585mm) – 65in (1,651mm), depending on body style. Kerb weight (typical) 2,900lb (1,315kg).

Commando (1972-1973)
As for Jeepster Commando, except as follows:
Engine: 232ci (3,801cc) OHV six-cylinder with 3.75in (95.25mm) bore and 3.5in (88.9mm) stroke, 8.0:1 compression ratio, single-barrel carburettor, 100bhp at 3,600rpm and 185lb.ft at 1,800rpm; standard.

258ci (4,228cc) OHV six-cylinder with 3.75in (95.25mm) bore and 3.9in (99.06mm) stroke, 8.0:1 compression ratio, single-barrel carburettor, 110bhp at 3,500rpm and 195lb.ft at 2,000rpm;

optional.

304ci (4,982cc) OHV V8 with 3.75in (95.25mm) bore and 3.44in (87.38mm) stroke, 8.4:1 compression ratio, two-barrel carburettor, 150bhp at 4,200rpm and 245lb.ft at 2,500rpm; optional.

Dimensions: Wheelbase 104in (2,642mm). Front track 51.5in (1,308mm). Rear track 50in 1,270mm). Length 174.5in (4,432mm). Kerb weight (typical) 3,000lb (1,361kg).

Cherokee (1974-1983)

As for contemporary Wagoneer, except as follows:
Engines: 258ci six-cylinder standard; 360ci V8 with two-barrel carburettor optional; 360 V8 with four-barrel carburettor optional; 401ci V8 with four-barrel carburettor optional 1974-78.
Steering and brakes: Unassisted steering and unassisted all-drum brakes 1974-77; power-assisted brakes with discs on front wheels 1978-83. Variable-ratio power-assisted steering optional 1978-83.
Dimensions: Front track 65.4in (1,661mm) wide-track models. Rear track 62.3in (1,582mm) wide-track models. Kerb weight (typical) 4,025lb (1,825kg).

CJ-7 (1976-1986)

Engines: 232ci (3,801cc) OHV six-cylinder with 3.75in (95.25mm) bore and 3.5in (88.9mm) stroke, 8:1 compression ratio, single-barrel carburettor, 100bhp at 3,600rpm and 185lb.ft at 1,800rpm; standard 1976-80.

258ci (4,228cc) OHV six-cylinder with 3.75in (95.25mm) bore and 3.9in (99.06mm) stroke, 8.0:1 compression ratio, single-barrel carburettor (1976-78) or two-barrel carburettor (1979-86), 110bhp at 3,500rpm and 195lb.ft at 2,000rpm (1976-78) or 114bhp at 3,200rpm and 210lb.ft at 2,000rpm (1979-86); optional 1972-86.

304ci (4,982cc) OHV V8 with 3.75in (95.25mm) bore and 3.44in (87.38mm) stroke, 8.4:1 compression ratio, four-barrel (1976-78) or two-barrel (1979-81) carburettor, 150bhp at 4,200rpm and 245lb.ft at 2,500rpm (1976-78) or 130bhp at 3,200rpm and 225lb.ft at 2,200rpm (1979-81); optional 1976-81.

151ci (2,474cc) Hurricane (Pontiac Iron Duke) OHV four-cylinder with 4in (101.6mm) bore and 3in (76.2mm) stroke, 8.2:1 compression ratio, two-barrel carburettor, 86bhp at 4,000rpm and 125lb.ft at 2,600rpm; standard 1980-83.

150ci (2,464cc) OHV four-cylinder with 3.876in (98.45mm) bore and 3.188in (80.98mm) stroke, 9.13:1 compression ratio, two-barrel carburettor, 105bhp at 5,000rpm and 132lb.ft at 2,800rpm; standard 1984-86.
Transmission: Three-speed all-synchromesh gearbox (standard 1976-81); gear ratios 3.00:1, 1.83:1, 1.00:1. Three-speed Turbo-

Hydramatic automatic (optional 1976-79); gear ratios 2.48:1, 1.48:1, 1.00:1. Four-speed gearbox with synchromesh on second, third and fourth gears; gear ratios 6.32:1, 3.00:1, 1.69:1, 1.00:1 (optional 1977-83). Three-speed Torque-Flite automatic (optional 1980-86); gear ratios 2.74:1, 1.55:1, 1.00:1. Four-speed all-synchromesh gearbox (standard 1982-86); gear ratios 4.07:1, 2.39:1, 1.49:1, 1.00:1. Five-speed all-synchromesh gearbox (optional 1982-86); gear ratios 4.07:1, 2.39:1, 1.49:1, 1.00:1, 0.83:1. Two-speed transfer gearbox with selectable four-wheel drive on manual models; low ratio 2.03:1 (1976-79), 2.62:1 (1980-86). Quadra-Trac permanent four-wheel drive with optional low ratio (2.57:1) standard with automatic gearbox, 1976-80. Axle ratio 3.54:1 standard and 4.09:1 optional (1976-80); 3.54:1 standard and 3.73:1 optional (1981-86, four-cylinder models); 2.73:1 standard and 3.31:1 optional (1981-86, six-cylinder models).
Steering, suspension and brakes: Cam-and-lever steering. Semi-elliptic leaf springs all round with hydraulic dampers. Drum brakes 1976-77; front disc brakes with power assistance 1978-86.
Dimensions: Wheelbase 93.5in (2,375mm). Front track 54in (1,372mm). Rear track 52.5in (1,333mm). Length 147.9in (3,757mm). Width 65.3in (1,659mm). Height 67.6in (1,717mm). Kerb weight (typical) 2,680lb (1,216kg).

CJ-8 Scrambler (1981-1986)

As for contemporary CJ-7, except as follows:
Dimensions: Wheelbase 103.4in (2,626mm). Length 177.2in (4,501mm). Height 69.2in (1,758mm). Kerb weight (typical) 2,759 lb (1,251kg).

XJ Cherokee and Wagoneer Limited (from 1984)

Engines: 150ci (2,464cc) OHV four-cylinder with 3.876in (98.45mm) bore and 3.188in (80.98mm) stroke, 9.13:1 compression ratio (1984-85) or 9.2:1 (from 1986); two-barrel carburettor (1984-85) or throttle-body fuel injection (1986-90) or sequential multi-point electronic fuel injection (from 1991); 105bhp at 5,000rpm and 132lb.ft at 2,800rpm (1984-85), 117bhp at 5,000rpm and 135lb.ft at 3,000rpm (1986-90), 121bhp (1987-90), 130bhp at 5,000rpm and 149lb.ft at 3,000rpm (from 1991); standard.

173ci (2,835cc) OHV V6, with 3.5in (88.9mm) bore and 2.99in (75.9mm) stroke, 8.5:1 compression ratio, electronic fuel injection, 110bhp at 4,800rpm and 145lb.ft at 2,100rpm; optional 1984-87.

241ci (3,960cc) OHV six-cylinder with 98.4mm bore and 87mm stroke, 8.75:1 compression ratio, sequential multi-point electronic fuel injection, 173bhp at 4,500rpm and 220lb.ft at 2,500rpm (1987), 177bhp (1988), 190bhp (1991-92); 174bhp at 4,600rpm and

222lb.ft at 2,400rpm (from 1993); optional from 1987.

126ci (2,068cc) four-cylinder turbocharged indirect-injection diesel with 86mm bore and 89mm stroke, 21.5:1 compression ratio, 82bhp at 4,000rpm and 132.5lb.ft at 2,250rpm; optional 1986-94 (1987 only in USA).

152ci (2,499cc) four-cylinder turbocharged indirect-injection diesel with 92mm bore and 94mm stroke, 20.9:1 compression ratio, 116bhp at 4,000rpm (114bhp at 3,900rpm from 1998) and 205lb.ft at 1,800rpm (221lb.ft at 2,000rpm from 1998); optional in Europe from 1994.

Transmission: Four-speed manual primary gearbox standard on four-cylinder models; four-speed automatic optional from 1994; five-speed manual standard on all six-cylinder and diesel types; three-speed automatic optional on six-cylinders (1984-86); four-speed overdrive automatic optional on six-cylinders from 1987. Gear ratios (four-speed manual) 3.93:1, 2.33:1, 1.45:1, 1.00:1; (three-speed automatic) 2.74:1, 1.55:1, 1.00:1; (four-speed automatic) 2.80:1, 1.53:1, 1.00:1, 0.75:1; (five-speed manual, petrol) 3.93:1, 2.33:1, 1.45:1, 1.00:1, 0.85:1; (five-speed manual, diesel) 4.31:1, 2.3:1, 1.44:1, 1.00:1, 0.79:1. Two-speed transfer gearbox with Command-Trac selectable four-wheel drive; Selec-Trac automatic selectable four-wheel drive optional (standard on some models). Trac-Lok limited-slip rear differential. Rear-wheel drive only available. Axle ratio 3.31:1 standard and 3.73:1 optional (1984-87); 3.55:1 (4-litre); 3.73:1 (2.5-litre turbodiesel); 4.11:1 (2.5-litre petrol).

Steering, suspension and brakes: Recirculating-ball steering with power assistance as standard. Live front axle with coil springs and Quadra-Link four locating arms, anti-roll bar and gas dampers; live rear axle with semi-elliptic leaf springs, anti-roll bar and gas dampers (no rear anti-roll bar on 2.5-litre turbodiesel models). Disc front brakes (ventilated from 1997) and drum rear brakes; power assistance standard; ABS optional and standard on some models from 1989.

Dimensions: Wheelbase 101.4in (2,575mm). Front and rear track 58in (1,473mm). Length 165.3in (4,198mm). Width 70.5in (1,791mm). Height 63.3in (1,608mm). Kerb weight (typical) 2,886lb (1,309kg), four-cylinder petrol; 2,971lb (1,348kg), V6 petrol; 3,600lb (1,633kg), 4-litre six-cylinder.

Comanche (1985-1992)

As for XJ Cherokee, except as follows:

Engines: 150ci four-cylinder standard; 173ci V6 optional 1986 only; 4-litre six-cylinder optional from 1987.

Transmission: Four-speed primary gearbox on four-cylinder models, 1986-88; five-speed on all six-cylinder types and on four-cylinders from 1989. Three-speed automatic optional on 1986

models; four-speed automatic optional with six-cylinder engine from 1987. Two-speed transfer gearbox with Selec-Trac selectable four-wheel drive on 1986 models; Command-Trac selectable four-wheel drive optional in 1986 and standard from 1987. Rear-wheel drive only optional.

Dimensions: Wheelbase 112.9in (2,868mm), 4x4 short-bed; 113.1in (2,873mm), 4x2 short-bed; 119.4in (3,033mm), 4x4 long-bed; 119.6in (3,038mm), 4x2 long-bed. Length 179.3in (4,554mm), short-bed; 193.97in (4,927mm), long-bed. Width 71.7in (1,821mm). Height 64in (1,626mm). Kerb weight (typical) 3,025lb (1,372kg).

YJ Wrangler (1986-1996)

Engines: 150ci (2,464cc) OHV four-cylinder with 3.876in (98.45mm) bore and 3.188in (80.98mm) stroke, 9.13:1 compression ratio (later 9.2:1), sequential multi-point electronic fuel injection, 117bhp at 5,000rpm and 135lb.ft at 3,000rpm; standard.

258ci (4,228cc) OHV six-cylinder with 3.75in (95.25mm) bore and 3.9in (99.06mm) stroke, 8.0:1 compression ratio, two-barrel carburettor, 112bhp at 3,000rpm and 210lb.ft at 2,000rpm; optional 1986-89.

241ci (3,960cc) OHV six-cylinder with seven-bearing crankshaft, 98.4mm bore and 87mm stroke, 8.75:1 compression ratio, sequential multi-point electronic fuel injection, 174bhp at 4,600rpm and 222lb.ft at 2,400rpm; optional 1990-96.

Transmission: Five-speed all-synchromesh gearbox; gear ratios 4.07:1, 2.39:1, 1.49:1, 1.00:1, 0.83:1. Three-speed automatic optional with six-cylinder engines; gear ratios 2.74:1, 1.55:1, 1.00:1. Two-speed transfer gearbox with Command-Trac selectable four-wheel drive. Axle ratio 4.11:1 (four-cylinder) or 3.55:1 (six-cylinder).

Steering, suspension and brakes: Recirculating-ball steering with optional power assistance. Semi-elliptic leaf springs all round with hydraulic dampers; front anti-roll bar. Ventilated disc front and drum rear brakes with power assistance.

Dimensions: Wheelbase 93.4in. Front and rear track: 58in (1,475mm). Length 152in (3,860mm). Width 66in (1,676mm). Height 68.9in (1,750mm). Kerb weight (typical) 2,869lb (1,301kg) four-cylinder; 3,023lb (1371kg) six-cylinder.

ZJ Grand Cherokee and Grand Wagoneer (from 1992)

Engines: 241ci (3,960cc) OHV six-cylinder with 98.4mm bore and 87mm stroke, 8.75:1 compression ratio, multi-point sequential electronic fuel injection, 174bhp at 4,600rpm and 222lb.ft at 2,400rpm; standard.

318ci (5,216cc) OHV V8 with 99.34mm bore and 84.12mm

stroke, multi-point sequential electronic fuel injection, 215bhp at 4,750rpm and 285lb.ft at 3,050rpm; optional.

360ci (5,899cc) OHV V8 with 102mm bore and 91mm stroke, 8.7:1 compression ratio, multi-point sequential electronic fuel injection, 237bhp at 4,050rpm and 348lb.ft at 3,050rpm; optional from 1998.

152ci (2,499cc) four-cylinder turbocharged indirect-injection diesel with 92mm bore and 94mm stroke, 20.9:1 compression ratio, 116bhp at 4,000rpm (114bhp at 3,900rpm from 1998) and 205lb.ft at 1,800rpm (221lb.ft at 2,000rpm from 1998); optional for European markets from 1997.

Transmission: Five-speed manual or (except on turbodiesel models) four-speed overdrive automatic primary gearbox. Gear ratios (automatic) 2.45:1, 1.45:1, 1.00:1, 0.69:1. Two-speed transfer gearbox with Command-Trac selectable four-wheel drive, or (all V8 and Limited models) Quadra-Trac permanent four-wheel drive. Limited-slip rear differential; viscous-coupled central differential on models with permanent four-wheel drive. Axle ratio 3.55:1 (5.2-litre), 3.73:1 (2.5 turbodiesel, 4-litre and 5.9-litre).

Steering, suspension and brakes: Recirculating-ball steering with power assistance standard; variable ratio on some models. Live front and rear axles with coil springs, Quadra-Link four-link lateral location, anti-roll bar and gas dampers. Ventilated front disc brakes and rear drum brakes with power assistance and ABS standard; solid disc rear brakes optional and standard on some models; ventilated rear discs on 5.9-litre LX.

Dimensions: Wheelbase 105.9in (2,690mm). Front track 58.5in (1,486mm). Rear track 58.7in (1,491mm). Length 177.2in (4,500mm). Width 70.9in (1,800mm). Height 70in (1,778mm).

Kerb weight (typical) 3,990lb (1,810kg) 4-litre; 4,045lb (1,835kg) turbodiesel; 4,262lb (1,933kg) 5.9 LX.

TJ Wrangler (from 1997)
Engine: 150ci (2,464cc) OHV four-cylinder with five-bearing crankshaft, 3.876in (98.45mm) bore and 3.188in (80.98mm) stroke, 9.13:1 compression ratio (later 9.2:1), sequential multi-point electronic fuel injection, 117bhp at 5,200rpm and 136lb.ft at 3600rpm; standard.

241ci (3,960cc) OHV six-cylinder with seven-bearing crankshaft, 98.4mm bore and 87mm stroke, 8.75:1 compression ratio, sequential multi-point electronic fuel injection, 176bhp at 4,600rpm and 214lb.ft at 3,600rpm; optional.

Transmission: Five-speed all-synchromesh gearbox; gear ratios 3.93:1, 2.33:1, 1.45:1, 1.00:1, 0.85:1 (four-cylinder) or 3.83:1, 2.33:1, 1.44:1, 1.00:1, 0.79:1 (six-cylinder). Three-speed automatic optional with six-cylinder engines; gear ratios 2.74:1, 1.54:1, 1.00:1. Two-speed transfer gearbox with Command-Trac selectable four-wheel drive. Axle ratio 3.73:1 (four-cylinder) or 3.07:1 (six-cylinder).

Steering, suspension and brakes: Recirculating-ball steering with power assistance. Front and rear live axles with Quadra-Link four locating arms each; front and rear anti-roll bars; coil springs all round with hydraulic dampers. Ventilated disc front and drum rear brakes with power assistance.

Dimensions: Wheelbase 93.4in (2,372mm). Front and rear track 58in (1,473mm). Length 152.8in (3,883mm). Width 68.2in (1,732mm). Height 70.16in (1,782mm). Kerb weight (typical) 3,373lb (1,530kg), four-cylinder; 3,549lb (1,610kg), six-cylinder.

APPENDIX B

Production figures

Notes: 1. These figures are arranged **in chronological order of the models' introduction.** Where two models were introduced in the same year, alphabetical order is used, eg CJ-5A precedes DJ-5A.

2. Some production numbers are simply not available. The main gaps are between 1962 and 1973, when records of individual model totals were not kept (or, at least, have not yet been found). According to the Chrysler Historical Collection, 'it is generally assumed that Jeep production figures will never be positively determined'.

Willys Quad		**1940**
1940	2 (prototypes only)	

MA		**1941**
1941	1,555	

MB		**1941-1945**
1941-1945	361,339	

(Note: of these, 25,808 were the early 'slat-grille' model and 335,531 had the pressed-steel grille.) A further 277,896 examples were built by Ford as the Ford GPW between 1942 and 1945.

CJ-2A   1945-1949

1945	1824	1948	62,861
1946	71,455	1949	104
1947	77,958	(*Total:* 214,202)	

Station Wagon and Utility Wagon   1946-1965
Panel Delivery and Sedan Delivery   1947-1963

1946	6,534	1955	21,875
1947	27,515	1956	14,970
1948	44,381	1957	13,493
1949	37,547	1958	9,248
1950	39,911	1959	14,340
1951	36,995	1960	16,440
1952	12,069	1961	11,429
1953	18,811	1962-65	Figures not available
1954	7,116		

Jeep Truck   1947-1965
(Figures in brackets denote two-wheel-drive versions and are included in the overall totals.)

1947	4,988	(2,642)	1956	16,654	(4)
1948	30,173	(9,216)	1957	9,594	(0)
1949	15,712	(5,955)	1958	8,445	(0)
1950	18,634	(5,650)	1959	11,742	(0)
1951	38,047	(19,704)	1960	14,636	(275)
1952	16,155	(0)	1961	3,546	(0)
1953	16,498	(0)	1962 -1965	Figures not available	
1954	4,477	(0)			
1955	13,856	(0)			

CJ-3A   1948-1953

1948	309	1951	40,121
1949	31,491	1952	34,654
1950	24,060	1953	1,208
		(*Total:* 131,843)	

Jeepster   1948-1950
(*Note:* Some unsold 1950 models were sold as 1951-model Jeepsters.)

1948	10,326	1950	5,845
1949	2,961	(*Total:* 19,132)	

MC (M-38)   1950-1953

1950	1,563	1952	22,972
1951	13,317	1953	23,571
		(*Total:* 61,423)	

CJ-3B   1952-1968

1952	2,360	1961	1,147
1953	33,047	1962	9,416
1954	35,972	1963	9,801
1955	12,567	1964	5,271
1956	10,145	1965	2,847
1957	5,756	1966	5,459
1958	6,178	1967	2,523
1959	5,420	1968	1,446
1960	6,139	(*Total:*155,494)	

MD (M-38A1)   1952-1971

1952	*	1962	2,957
1953	*29,769	1963	4,369
1954	9,560	1964	2,622
1955	8,826	1965	578
1956	3,166	1966	320
1957	1,050	1967	840
1958	780	1968	1,906
1959	1,273	1969	0
1960	2,673	1970	0
1961	2,064	1971	596

* 1952 production included in 1953 figure.

                  (*Total:* 101,488)

MDA   1953-1967

1953	2	1961	0
1954	1,722	1962	1,155
1955	2,271	1963	464
1956	0	1964	0
1957	0	1965	43
1958	0	1966	77
1959	0	1967	147
1960	0	(*Total:* 5,881)	

CJ-5   1954-1983

1954	3,883	1970	13,518
1955	23,595	1971	12,559
1956	18,441	1972	22,601
1957	20,819	1973	30,449
1958	12,401	1974	43,087
1959	17,488	1975	32,486
1960	19,753	1976	31,116
1961	2,064	1977	32,996
1962	14,072	1978	37,611
1963	12,499	1979	41,501
1964	16,029	1980	24,574

1965	21,014	1981	13,477	1978	28,871	1988	14,117
1966	17,974	1982	6,080	1979	27,437	1989	10,159
1967	18,186	1983	3,085	1980	10,481	1990	6,449
1968	19,683			1981	13,741	1991	1,560
1969	20,262	(*Total:* 603,303)		1982	18,709	1992	330

CJ-6   1955-1981

1955	581	1969	2,433
1956	2,523	1970	2,234
1957	1,236	1971	1,806
1958	1,387	1972	1,175
1959	1,947	1973	1,720
1960	2,201	1974	2,826
1961	244	1975	2,935
1962	2,502	1976	2,431
1963	1,534	1977	2,754
1964	1,702	1978	743
1965	2,062	1979	992
1966	3,521	1980	1,633
1967	2,295	1981	360
1968	2,395	(*Total:* 50,172)	

Gladiator   1963-1970
J-series   1971-1987

1963-1973 Figures not available		1981	8,048
1974	15,524	1982	6,113
1975	13,958	1983	4,705
1976	16,188	1984	3,082
1977	17,252	1985	1,953
1978	20,495	1986	1,515
1979	18,966	1987	1,153
1980	6,839		

DJ-3A   1955-1965

1955	1,316	1961	199
1956	1,491	1962	1,326
1957	1,248	1963	1,123
1958	1,175	1964	809
1959	2,509	1965	50
1960	2,360	(*Total:* 13,606)	

CJ-5A   1964-1967

1964	4,128	1966	1,190
1965	1,987	1967	89
		(*Total:* 7,394)	

CJ-6A   1964-1967

1964	164	1966	160
1965	115	1967	20
		(*Total:* 459)	

FC-150   1957-1965

1957	6,637	1960	1,925
1958	2,072	1961	1,298

1959 *Figures not available   1962-1965 Figures not available
* See FC-170

DJ-5A   1964-1973

1964	1	1969	386
1965	1,316	1970	254
1966	443	1971	153
1967	1,042	1972	87
1968	521	1973	102
		(*Total:* 4,305)	

FC-170   1957-1965

1957	3,101	1960	3,004
1958	1,522	1961	2,373
1959*	1,546	1962-1965 Figures not available	

*1959 figures are for FC-150 and FC-170 production combined.

DJ-6A   1965-1973

1965	168	1970	467
1966	720	1971	949
1967	791	1972	141
1968	627	1973	23
1969	467		
		(*Total:* 4,353)	

Wagoneer   1963-1992

1963-1973 Figures not available		1983	18,478
1974	13,746	1984	20,019
1975	16,708	1985	17,814
1976	21,912	1986	17,254
1977	20,298	1987	14,265

Jeepster Commando C-101   1966-1971
Commando C-104   1972-1973

1966	2,345	1970	9,268
1967	12,621	1971	7,903
1968	13,924	1972	10,685
1969	11,289	1973	9,538
		(*Total:* 77,573)	

Cherokee   1974-1983

1974	14,082	1979	39,183
1975	16,294	1980	7,614
1976	26,365	1981	6,321
1977	33,684	1982	6,911
1978	40,698	1983	6,186
			(*Total*: 197,238)

CJ-7   1976-1986

1976	21,061	1982	23,820
1977	25,414	1983	37,673
1978	38,274	1984	42,644
1979	55,264	1985	43,315
1980	38,183	1986	25,939
1981	27,787		
		(*Total*: 379,354)	

CJ-8 Scrambler   1981-1986

1981	8,355	1984	4,130
1982	7,759	1985	2,015
1983	5,405	1986	128
		(*Total*: 27,792)	

Cherokee and Wagoneer Limited   1984 on

1984	93,326	1991	151,578
1985	120,328	1992	137,826
1986	107,225	1993	144,961
1987	139,295	1994	166,094
1988	187,136	1995	172,282
1989	207,216	1996	164,332
1990	151,230	1997	184,888

Comanche   1985-1992

1985	29,245	1989	25,311
1986	33,386	1990	9,576
1987	43,070	1991	5,188
1988	43,718	1992	952
		(*Total*: 190,446)	

Wrangler (YJ)   1986-1995

1986	16,853	1992	59,690
1987	36,114	1993	72,903
1988	52,691	1994	78,222
1989	69,565	1995	83,374
1990	58,184		
1991	65,135	(*Total*: 592,731)	

Grand Cherokee and Grand Wagoneer   1992 on

1992	121,333	1995	320,465
1993	246,156	1996	346,376
1994	262,476	1997	308.275

Wrangler (TJ)   1996 on

1996	92,340	1997	107,053

Overall annual production figures

Note: The upheavals caused by various changes of ownership at Jeep have made it impossible to establish a definitive set of production figures. These figures are the best that can be achieved at present. They do not include military or government production.

1945	1,824	1970	86,254	1995	575,171
1946	78,808	1971	53,051	1996	602,931
1947	97,581	1972	71,205	1997	600,216
1948	159,002	1973	94,035		
1949	86,151	1974	93,317		
1950	90,424	1975	108,612		
1951	119,200	1976	126,125		
1952	57,879	1977	139,140		
1953	75,759	1978	180,514		
1954	46,002	1979	134,624		
1955	64,166	1980	62,841		
1956	64,267	1981	92,248		
1957	64,639	1982	75,269		
1958	43,303	1983	75,534		
1959	52,483	1984	176,276		
1960	67,842	1985	225,914		
1961	49,073	1986	207,514		
1962	85,457	1987	248,930		
1963	110,549	1988	308,564		
1964	120,868	1989	319,149		
1965	108,574	1990	229,327		
1966	99,623	1991	226,209		
1967	116,744	1992	323,233		
1968	117,573	1993	463,401		
1969	93,160	1994	501,392		

APPENDIX C

Performance figures

Note: It would be impossible to quote detailed performance figures for every model of Jeep in the space available, even if such figures existed. Early road tests often did not quote performance figures because they were irrelevant to the Jeep's purpose, and in the 1970s and early 1980s many US magazines ducked the issue in an attempt to be politically correct. The figures given here are therefore intended to be representative only. Dates quoted refer to model-year.

Year and model	0-60mph	Max. speed	Source
i) CJs and derivatives			
1960 CJ-6 with Hurricane 4-cyl	N/A	61.3mph	*Wheels*
1969 Jeepster Convertible V6 automatic	12.6sec	87mph	*Car Life*
1971 CJ-5 with 225ci V6	11.2sec	92mph	*4WD*
1972 CJ-5 with 304ci V8	13.0sec	82mph	*4WD*
1972 Commando with 258ci six	14.2sec	75mph approx.	*Track and Traffic*
1978 CJ-7 Golden Eagle 304ci V8 auto	11.4sec	84mph	*PV4*
1980 CJ-5 Renegade with 151ci 4-cylinder	18.0sec	75mph	*PV4*
1982 CJ-5 with 258ci six	12.2sec	70mph	*PV4*
1997 Wrangler 2.5 manual	13.6sec	92mph	Chrysler Jeep
1997 Wrangler 4.0 manual	8.8sec	112mph	Chrysler Jeep
1997 Wrangler 4.0 auto	9.5sec	109mph	Chrysler Jeep
ii) Senior Jeeps			
1946 Station Wagon with Go-Devil 4-cylinder	N/A	65mph	Willys Overland
1959 Utility Wagon with Super Hurricane 6-cyl	N/A	75mph	*Car Life*
1961 Utility Wagon with Hurricane 4-cylinder	26.6sec	60mph+	*Motor Trend*
1963 Wagoneer with 230ci six	16.1sec	90mph	*Motor Trend*
1966 Wagoneer with 327ci V8 and auto	14.5sec	80mph +	*Canada Track and Traffic*
1967 Wagoneer with 232ci six	19.7sec	84.5mph	*Car South Africa*
1971 Wagoneer with 350ci V8 and auto	12.9sec	91mph	*Road and Track*
1973 Wagoneer with 360ci V8 and auto	12.3sec	85mph approx.	*Driving*
1974 Cherokee S with 401ci V8 and auto	10.0sec	90mph	*PV4*
1980 Cherokee with 258ci six	15.6sec	86mph	*PV4*
1985 Cherokee 2.1 Turbo diesel	20.06sec	N/A	*Four Wheeler*
1997 Cherokee 2.5 manual	12.1sec	102.5mph	Chrysler Jeep
1997 Cherokee 2.5 Turbo diesel	13.1sec	102.5mph	Chrysler Jeep
1997 Cherokee 4.0 auto	9.5sec	112mph	Chrysler Jeep
1997 Grand Cherokee 2.5 Turbo diesel	14.0sec	96mph	Chrysler Jeep
1997 Grand Cherokee 4.0	10.9sec	112mph	Chrysler Jeep
1997 Grand Cherokee 5.2	8.1sec	116mph	Chrylser Jeep
1998 Grand Cherokee 5.9	7.9sec	125mph	Chrysler Jeep
iii) Commercials			
1965 J-200 with 230ci six	20.0sec	80.8mph	*Car South Africa*
1978 J-20 130.7-in with 2-bbl 360 V8	14.1sec	82mph	*PV4*